Y0-BXV-147

Making
Money
TYPING
AT HOME

Also by Peggy Glenn:

WORD PROCESSING PROFITS AT HOME   ($15.95)

PUBLICITY FOR BOOKS AND AUTHORS   ($12.95)

and

KEROSENE HEATERS: A Consumer's Review   ($3.95)

DON'T GET BURNED! A Family Fire-Safety Guide   ($7.95)

   (above book co-written with her husband, Gary A. Glenn)

Peggy Glenn's

Complete
Business
Manual for

Making Money TYPING · AT HOME

Aames-Allen
■ PUBLISHING COMPANY ■

■ 1106 Main Street ■
Huntington Beach, CA 92648

MAKING MONEY TYPING AT HOME

by Peggy Glenn
foreword by Alma Vanasse, M.A.

Aames-Allen Publishing Co.
1106 Main Street
P.O. Box 453
Huntington Beach   CA 92648   USA
714/536-4926

Printed in the United States of America.
Delta Lithograph, Inc., Van Nuys, California.

Acknowledgement is made to the following for reprinted
materials: p. 152, Dennis the Menace cartoon by permission
of Hank Ketcham and © by Field Enterprises, Inc.,[T.M.]

Library of Congress Cataloging in Publication (CIP) Data

CONTENTS

DEDICATED

to all who have put forth super-human
effort to help me finish this book...

and all who will read it and consider
my human-ness if a "typo" is found...

and to Gary, my love.

FOREWORD

The benefits to individuals who choose to work out of their homes are many—if the original plans for the business are well thought out. Peggy Glenn has written this very useful guide to help a beginner. The book has been written in a very professional way and includes many necessary details.

Peggy Glenn understands the needs of individuals (especially homemakers) and she has explored the most efficient way for them to launch their own careers. Novices will feel confident that they are following a tried and true method when they use her book to help set up their own home typing business (or as a guide for a different home-based business).

In addition to helping individuals set up their own home businesses, Peggy Glenn is willing to help people establish their own network system to support each other. This is a very powerful aid to this special group.

There are many creative individuals in their homes who have great ideas but lack the impetus to begin their venture. This book of Peggy Glenn's will fill the void that has existed because it has almost every answer to the questions: Where? Why? and How do I begin?

Alma Vanasse, M.A.
Career Guidance Specialist

Director, Women's Center
Saddleback College
Mission Viejo, California

v

ACKNOWLEDGEMENT

I'm indebted to a great many people for the faith they've shown in me and the patience and help they've given me in putting together this book.

Without the loyalty, encouragement, and assistance of my family, professional colleagues, and close friends, you wouldn't be reading this. <u>I</u> know who they are, <u>they</u> know who they are, and you <u>wouldn't</u> know who they are, so I won't mention all their names. For satisfaction of my own need to say "thanks", however, I must mention: my husband, Gary, whose love and support were always there; and Shasta Glenn, Jane Allison, Joe Flinn, Barbara Seese, Bernie Petitjean, Pat Blakeley, Barbara Erickson, Mindy Gaunt, Joan Woolard, and Ann Powell, Nancy Martin, Gene Hinze.

I owe a great deal to my parents and grandparents who instilled in me a long time ago a respect for words, whether I read them or wrote them, and a love of education. They gave me the time and opportunity to express myself, even when they disagreed with me. I was never without books or a library, and I'm grateful to be able to contribute to someone else's library now.

I also acknowledge you, the reader, and all who have read earlier editions. We do feel our worth, we will be successful, and we will elevate the image of the professional person who types (or word processes) at home.

CHAPTER 1
Introduction

WHAT'S THIS BOOK ALL ABOUT, WHO IS IT FOR

This book is intended for your use in setting up a successful home-based typing business and running it for as long as it makes you happy. The information in this book can be applied whether you intend to run a small part-time business, or whether you plan on running a full-time business.

While most of the information in this book is geared toward working in your home, the basic business advice will be appropriate even if you choose to rent a small office away from your home. You can earn a living typing at home if you possess the following: good typing and general-office skills, professional-quality equipment, and a supply of customers.

I assume that you can type. As a general rule, if you can complete a single page of double-spaced pica typing in ten minutes with only three or four errors, your typing skill level is adequate. I also assume that you have done general office work and are familiar with common business correspondence guidelines. You should be able to set up a letter and envelope and/or a report or proposal without asking for your client's advice. This is the very minimum qualifications. If your typing and/or general office skills are not at the level I just described, take a short refresher course through the adult education deparment in your local school district, or enroll in a typing course at a community college.

If what you lack is current knowledge of office procedures -- maybe you've been away from the job world for a number of years -- try easing back into the profession by accepting temporary work through an agency. This approach doesn't involve the demoralizing ritual of looking for, interviewing for, and having to leave permanent employment. With a temporary agency as the intermediary, either you or the employer is free to terminate the work relationship with no unpleasant confrontation.

The most rewarding and fulfilling aspect of a home-based typing business is that you are free to work whenever it is convenient for YOU: morning, afternoon, evenings, weekends, or any combination of hours or days. Irregular work schedules -- yours or a family member's -- are more easily managed. You are also free to pursue personal activities.

The income is pleasant, too. Whether you earn money for extras, to help out with inflation's erosion of your lifestyle, or as your only source of revenue, you can see a direct correlation between how hard you work and how much money you earn. You work to support you and your goals. You're not just another payroll number or body at a desk at some large company or obscure governmental agency.

IS THERE ENOUGH WORK FOR EVERYONE?

In most all areas of the country, there is plenty of work to go around. Just as there are many pizza parlors, auto repair shops, and grocery stores, so will there be many services such as yours providing business support. As you will see when you read later chapters of this book, many of these typing firms will specialize. Each of these will be unique. Don't be afraid of competition. Instead, develop a sense of cooperation. Network with other typists in your area, referring customers within the network whenever there is a match between the kind of work you do and the kind of work the customer needs done. You'll see that this personal referral is better than losing customers to inferior typists. The public image of all who render any kind of administrative or secretarial support will be greatly improved by this referral process.

A natural spirit of competitive cooperation within a local group of typists will be beneficial to all. The work will retain a high quality. Yes, of course, you feel you're the best -- you should feel that way. That high degree of self-confidence will be reflected in all your contacts with customers and may be just the "extra" that will land you a job or contract. But retain some humility with that confidence. Realize that you can't possibly do all the work there is; someone else has to do some of it.

If there are three or four of you working in a particular area, get to know one another. Once you know each other, you may find that there are subtle differences in your skills and in the work you each like to do. These differences will help you determine just which typist is perfect for which customer when you need a referral. Conversely, if another typist wants to refer a customer to you, if she or he knows your particular strengths, both you and the customer will be happy.

In my area there were over two dozen typists to whom I referred customers. These typists returned the favor as well. For instance, my strong area was academic typing, and I was especially strong in a few subject areas. If I received a request to type a psychology, nursing, or education paper, for example, I took it on gladly. However, if I got a math, chemistry, or computer science paper, I referred it to one of my colleagues.

As another example, most of my work experience had been at colleges and universities and most of a colleague's experience had been in the business world of property investment companies, real estate firms, accountants, and financial firms. We both advertised our typing businesses; and sometimes customers didn't look beyond our names to see what kind of work we specialized in. So we traded customers and everyone was happier. The customer knew that he or she could expect the same professional work from all of us. That gave us good public relations and kept customers coming back over and over again.

WHAT'S THIS BUSINESS ALL ABOUT?

Do you believe myths? The two most common myths about small businesses -- and particularly home-based small businesses -- are:

1.   It's complicated.

Not so, it requires some time, some thought, some planning, some intuition, but it's not complicated.

2.   It's only for the very smart or very rich.

Not so again. Some of the richest people don't have the slightest idea about what makes a good idea work, nor do they have the "street" skills to make it work.

And some of the most intelligent people don't have
enough inner drive or common sense to follow through on
a plan.

Cottage industries -- another term for home-based
businesses -- have experienced unprecedented growth
over the last 15 years, and especially during the last
4-5 years. A few years ago, most cottage industries
were small, very part-time businesses that folks worked
at in their spare time for supplemental income. Today,
home-based businesses are more likely to be full-time
businesses that folks use as their sole means of support. Lately, everyone from economists to sociologists
and urban planners are heralding the cottage industry
as the work wave of the future.

Women represent a substantial percentage of these
home-based businesses. A recent United States Chamber
of Commerce report states that, "Fifteen million businesses in the United States file IRS reports under
Schedule C (sole proprietor). Only 5 million of those
businesses (that's less than one-third, friends) list
an address away from home. The other 10 million list
home addresses. Many of those businesses are operated
by women."

Personally, I see home-based typists or freelance
secretaries as the way of the future in a lot of areas.
I firmly believe that the demand will increase for
skilled typists who can produce written documents of
superior quality at reasonable rates. Just as word
processors are helping to cut costs in business and
industry, many major companies are using every available method to trim their payroll and benefits
expenses. Businesses are much more willing to hire
outside help on an as-needed basis than they were a
decade ago.

Some companies try to solve their workload problems by hiring temporary employees when there's a work
crunch or when a permanent employee is out for an
extended period of time. However, a company that contracts for temporary help through an employment agency
pays on the average of $4 per hour more for a temporary
employee than they pay one of their own salaried employees.. Yet the person who is hired through an agency as
a temporary employee is probably paid at or slightly
below the regular employee's scale. This is how the
temporary agency makes its profit.

4

So why don't you eliminate the middleman? Be an
independent contractor, your own boss. Become a
reliable temporary employee to businesses, lawyers,
doctors and medical labs, people who are going to college and need papers typed, and writers who hate to
face the typewriter to make the final copy of a manuscript. Work at their place or at your home.

Be a **PROFESSIONAL**! Think of yourself as a **PRO-
FESSIONAL**! Conduct yourself as a **PROFESSIONAL**! Before
long you'll be **paid** as a professional, **treated** as one,
and be able to get Lloyds of London to insure your
hands and fingers (or whatever you type with).

The first step in the process is to look closely
at: your reasons for starting your own business, your
personality, your budget, and your family situation and
any special circumstances. Don't be shy, and don't be
superficial. Take a good hard look as Chapter 1 tells
you how.

*   *   *   *

P.S. I assume that the majority of people who will
read this book are women. If you are a man, please
don't take offense, and please know that I am well
aware that many men are excellent typists and well-
qualified to run home-based businesses. Popular experience dictates that this book be directed to the female
audience just as a book on fixing motorcycles will probably be directed at males. Consider my dilemma at
making this whole thing non-sexist, and if you are a
man, please accept the female orientation of this text.

P.S. #2 Before we go any further, I'd also like to
mention that this book has been typed for you, over the
objections of most everyone in the publishing industry
who maintain that a quality book should be typeset.
But I know you, my reader. You're like me, and we're
used to reading typewritten material in just this large
format. BUT, looks can be deceiving. This book was
"typed" on my word processor to save countless hours of
tedious editing and revising and retyping. Fooled you,
but only because I care about you. Happy reading.

Thanks,

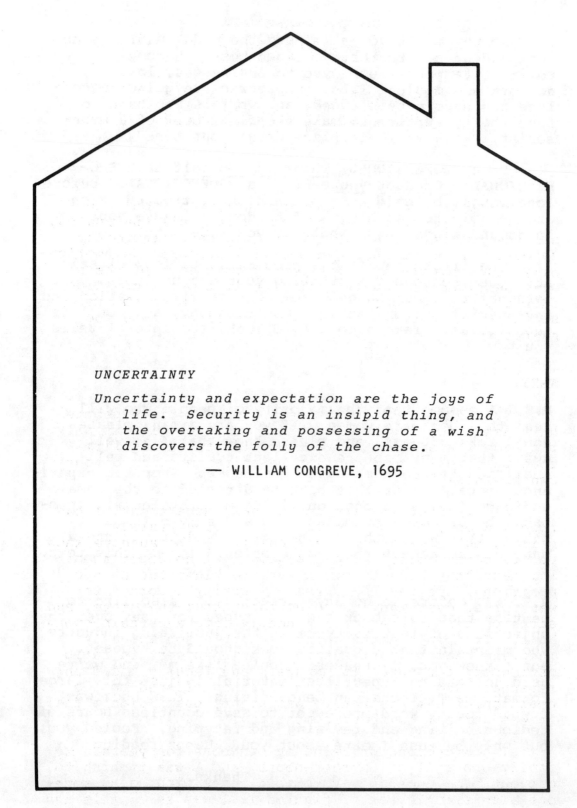

UNCERTAINTY

*Uncertainty and expectation are the joys of
    life. Security is an insipid thing, and
    the overtaking and possessing of a wish
    discovers the folly of the chase.*

— WILLIAM CONGREVE, 1695

CHAPTER 2
Getting Started

Whenever you start anything new, you should look closely and carefully at all the sides, all the angles, all the springboards and the roadblocks or temporary detours. Look at what can and will support you emotionally and financially? I hope you take each of these next sections seriously. If I've left out a question that applies to your life, YOU ask it. When you have satisfactory answers to all the questions, take the next step.

WHY?

It's difficult to estimate how many times people have asked me, "Why on earth did you ever give up all the security and benefits of working for a big firm that paid well and had great benefits to go into your own business?"

Well, after 7 years in the same department, I had received only one promotion, a few meager salary raises, but always more responsibility "because we know you're so capable." I had a good job, no doubt about it. But "the budget" was always to blame for no new positions. Beyond that, the university I worked for was spread over many campuses throughout the state, and each job classification fit neatly into a certain cubbyhole. It didn't matter what a clerk's job actually involved, each department was allowed a certain ratio of support personnel to managers and faculty based on revenue. Shortly before I quit, they offered me the position of Administrative Assistant, but I didn't feel it was worth it without combat pay!

I had dreamed of being my own boss for years. My family was full of entrepreneurs, and I was itching to get out from under the yoke that comes with being someone else's employee. I figured if I was as capable and smart as my superiors kept telling me I was, I ought to

be smart enough to get out of there and capitalize on
what I knew and could do, and how well I could do it.

A former head of career development at UCLA's
Placement and Career Planning Center once told a
reporter, "There are rare cases where a secretary ends
up being a vice president, but most secretaries stay
secretaries." I think that what I saw in the academic
world is true everywhere -- in business, in law, in
government, in medicine, in industry. Secretaries are
valued, but exploited. Many, like you and me, are
leaving. The shortage of qualified secretaries becomes
more critical each year.

Now, in my own business I have all the promotional
opportunity I'll ever need. In any given day I can be:

     "Go-fer"
     President
     Secretary
     Treasurer
     Receptionist
     Bill Collector
     Purchasing Agent
     Custodial Service
     Appointments Clerk
     Advertising Director, etc., etc., etc.

Another thing that bothered me when I was working
was watching the older secretaries -- some of whom had
been at the same job for many years -- taking medical
leaves and medical retirements in ever-increasing numbers. They were having heart attacks, open-heart sur-
gery, problems with high blood pressure, ulcers, etc.
I was young and didn't like the idea that I might meet
the same fate if I stayed there.

A recent study by the National Heart, Lung, and
Blood Institute found that the risk of heart disease is
twice as prevalent among working women who work in
clerical positions than in any other group of women,
working outside the home or not. The most vulnerable
were those clerical workers who had children at home.
Too much to do, in too little time, with too much
stress?

The study found that secretaries and other clerical workers had the highest degree of suppressed anger.
The women in the study also complained about unsuppor-
tive bosses, that they had almost no control over their
jobs, had no freedom of movement (needing permission to

leave their desk or use the rest room), and generally felt frustrated and powerless with no one to talk to about their problems. Those same feelings -- frustration, lack of control, no appreciation -- were part of my motivation.

Another big issue for me was family time. For example, in order to take time off when my children were ill, I had to lie to my employer. Tending to kids' illnesses wasn't a valid use of my sick time, so it was either lie or take the time without pay. In either case, guilt was the end result. Yes, I felt a responsibility to my job. Of course, I did. But I felt a much greater responsibility to my family. After awhile, I grew tired of arguing about it. I felt I needed more and more "mental health" days off. Was it burnout?

The last issue for me, and probably one that will fit the majority of working clerical women, was money. I really felt underpaid -- grossly exploited if you want the truth. Beyond that, by the time I deducted taxes and direct work expenses, it looked as if I were working for about $2 an hour. When I came to that "bottom line" it was "quittin' time." I was convinced I could make more money for less work and with less aggravation. I was right.

You can probably see that these feelings created a seething anger. You may be feeling that anger yourself. Please take my advice and deal with and resolve that anger before you plunge head-long into your business. If you don't, the first unpleasant or distressing encounter with a difficult customer will cause all those feelings to rush back, and you'll find yourself comparing the customer to the old boss or the old bureaucracy. This may be an unfair comparison. Allow yourself to forget the past situation. Then recognize that your new business will have trying times. When you find yourself boiling mad about an encounter with a particularly difficult customer, it will really help if you say out loud to yourself, "Maybe that guy was a drip, but this still beats working for someone else, because if he calls again, I won't have to work for him."

What personality traits or hidden wishes have you identified in yourself? Are you ambitious, willing to take a risk, feeling trapped in a corporate world, eager to take your idea and run with it? Go ahead and run. No one holds a stop-watch but you, but there are hundreds of fans on the sidelines watching you stride by and wishing they had the guts to run with you.

WHY NOT?

Another of my favorite answers to that question, "Why?" is usually another question: "Why not?" I know that's not a fair answer, but I mean it? Why shouldn't I have taken a chance? Why shouldn't you take your chance?

Several years ago I adopted a personal philosophy of having no "why-nots" or "what-ifs" in my life. I never wanted to look back and ask myself those questions or have regrets.

Some call it Yankee stubbornness, others call it selfishness. I prefer to think of myself as an incurable individualist. I want to do it my way, do what I like best, do it for the people I choose, and mesh my professional and personal lives with as much harmony as possible.

If I take on work and it turns out that I don't like the work or I don't care for the customer, I make up my mind to not accept that kind of job or that particular client again. If a customer is unpleasant, I'm simply too busy the next time he or she calls. I refuse graciously because I can't afford bad publicity, but I end up controlling my professional life. More about that process in Chapter 9.

Another big advantage for me was the freedom of choice in my wardrobe and working conditions. I prefer to wear sweat pants and t-shirts while sitting for hours at a keyboard. Occasionally if I wake up early, I'll even work a few hours in my robe and slippers. Now, you tell me an office where that would be appropriate? Oh, no, that's not the kind of attire that would readily be accepted out in the professional world of pantyhose, matched outfits, and color-coordinated accessories. But those early morning hours can be productive, and I had no dress code in my business.

No dress code, that is, unless I was seeing customers. I allowed customers to come to the office only with an appointment. I never greeted a customer when I was wearing the above-mentioned inappropriate attire of sweat pants or my robe and slippers. Now, I'll grant you that the customers were interested in the professional appearance of their finished typing project more than they were interestesd in the wardrobe of their typist, but there was more involved here than just the simple typing transaction. All of their business dealings with me would depend on their perception of my professionalism. If I needed to firmly discuss a bill they thought was too high, I needed to have been "seen" as a professional businesswoman from the start. How do you successfully argue over a $250 discrepancy when dressed in faded jeans and an oversize flannel shirt with the sleeves rolled up, or in shorts and a halter?

Occasionally a "veteran" customer would catch me in casual attire if they arrived during non-business hours. I didn't worry about it too much then. These rare occasions were only available to steady customers who already knew that I always did good work! And they appreciated that I was available evening hours. Sometimes I'd invite a special or long-standing customer to have a cup of coffee with us . . . no different than if my office were in the center of town or in a high-rise office building.

Minor illness presents less of a problem when working at home. A mild case of the flu, a cold, or an attack of the springtime sneezies no longer meant a day off from work, either. I may not have put in a full day, but there was no rule in my business that said I couldn't type for an hour or so, take a nap, and type some more.

When I had my "real job" I had to call in sick during those times . . . and you all know about calling in and telling the boss you're sick for the day. The news is not exactly greeted with enthusiasm. On the other hand, if someone who really should have stayed home comes in and sneezes all over the office, an entire office could be sidelined with a rotating flu-out. Ah-h-h, those guilt trips are just a memory now.

Examine your own life for "what-ifs" and "why-nots" and make the best choice for you.

DO YOU HAVE THE RIGHT PERSONALITY?

According to research conducted by the Small Business Administration and women's advocacy groups, there are certain personality traits in a woman that are necessary to insure that a self-employment venture will be profitable and successful.

Organization, dependability, self-motivation, confidence, perseverance, flexibility, authority, firmness, and tolerance are some of the key personality elements to look for in deciding if this kind of business is for you.

Organization and dependability are what will impress your customers and allow you to meet deadlines with a minimum of personal struggle. Self-motivation, confidence, and perseverance are what will keep you going when the business is slow and you have to rustle up more work.

Flexibility is an absolute must if you are to mesh your business and personal lives successfully. Authority, firmness, and an amazing amount of tolerance are essential in dealing with unpleasant customers under difficult circumstances.

If you are shy, easily-intimidated, self-doubting, or insecure, you will find it more difficult. This doesn't mean you can't try, and it doesn't automatically spell failure, but it definitely means you will have to work very hard. Perhaps simply recognizing these traits will help you overcome them or compensate for them.

Take a close look at your personality strengths and weaknesses. If you have a majority of positive traits and a minority of negative ones, self-employment is probably a worthwhile gamble for you. Try it and see.

HEED THESE WARNING SIGNALS

I do feel obligated to briefly discuss some very real "Why not's." I have talked with or heard from many women who tried their very best but were destined for failure before they started simply because their very best wasn't anywhere near good enough.

FIRST, be honest with yourself about your skills. If you repeatedly turn out work that looks messy, contains errors, or wasn't done on time or according to the directions, you will fail. Repeat customers is the backbone of this business; strong word-of-mouth referrals from old customers to new ones are the legs that support that backbone.

SECOND, be honest about your personality. If you're uncomfortable about meeting strangers, if you tremble at the thought of having customers come to your home, if you can't look a customer in the eye and tell him or her how much you charge, if you feel guilty when it's time to raise your prices, if you can't take a compliment, a home-based typing business is going to be a real struggle. The only way I see you overcoming this is to either deal by mail with writers or to hire a "front person" who will make all business contacts for you and a messenger who will pick up and deliver all work from clients.

THIRD, be honest about your family or social situation. You must have the support -- at least a little bit -- of the people who live in the same house with you, and even those close relatives who have a habit of telling you what, when, where, and how to run your life. If you live alone, be prepared for the difference between the camaraderie of working in an office and the solitude of working at home. Accept the workday loneliness if you like it (some people work best that way. I do), or develop extra social contacts if you'll miss that aspect of your work the most.

I'd like to recommend a few books which deal with the philosophy of working in the non-traditional way, and which also address the personality aspects of making self-employment successful. Unfortunately, a few of these may be out of print when you read this, and will be available only in libraries. But try to find them and enjoy reading them.

THE ENTREPRENEURIAL WOMAN, by Sandra Winston.
    Published by Newsweek Books and Bantam Books

WORKING FROM HOME, by Paul and Sarah Edwards.
    Published by Jeremy P. Tarcher, Inc.

MINDING MY OWN BUSINESS, by Marjorie McVicar and
    Julia Craig. Published by Richard Marek Publishers, Inc.

EARNING MONEY WITHOUT A JOB and
555 WAYS TO EARN EXTRA MONEY, by Jay Conrad
    Levinson. Published by Holt, Rinehart and
    Winston

BUDGET MATTERS

If you intend to use the home-based typing business for supplemental money or as a part-time job rather than as your sole means of support, the financial issues are not as critical for you. But read on anyway; much of this next part will be helpful to you.

If you are leaving a "real job" and setting up this business as your sole source of support, examine your budget carefully. Look for ways to save or to pare your current expenses. Carefully plan your cash flow so that you'll be able to pay all your bills.

FIRST, ask yourself these questions.

1.   How much actual cash do I need to make it from week to week, month to month? (Rent or mortgage, food, utilities, charge accounts, car payment, etc.)

2.   How much money is my "real job" costing me and can I save on any or all of those expenses? (Clothes, transportation, child care, fast foods, taxes, dues or fees, etc.)

3.   Do I have anything in the bank or credit union to get me over a rough spot, through a slow month, or to take care of unexpected bills? Do I have health insurance?

4.   Do I have to go into debt to set up, or can I do it on a pay-as-I-go basis? Do I have any credit in my own name? If I take a loan, will I be able to pay it back?

5.   Is there anyone else depending on my income?

6.   Can I be stingy with myself until the money starts coming in regularly? Can I set a budget and keep to it? Can I resist temptation and impulses and hang onto my money?

To plan your budget, take advantage of many excellent books in your local bookstore and library and/or pamphlets put out by the federal government. These give excellent advice on figuring a household budget, setting up a small business, and keeping track of all of the money -- coming in and going out.

Remember that nothing is forever. Refigure your income/outgo budget every six months. Your priorities may shift and you may find that one area needs adjusting to fit your new lifestyle.

My budgeting strategy was rather simple. I used my husband's paycheck to pay all the bills and we used my earnings to eat. With three teenagers to feed, that was motivation enough, believe me. The first steak was cause for celebration, and the first dinner in a restaurant was something like a Hollywood happening for us.

SECOND, small business experts advise that you set weekly income goals that are at least 25% higher than what you figure you MUST have. The income will fluctuate for a while, so in any week where you earn more than your goal, put the extra money aside to help you with a week that is under-goal.

THIRD, set aside 25% of what you earn according to the following formula: Mark 10% of your total earnings as sacred and absolutely untouchable. Deposit the money in some sort of interest-bearing account. This first 10% deduction should be used for paying insurance premiums, for taking your "benefits" (sick days, vacations, etc.), and as a small hedge against double-digit inflation.

Earmark a second 10% for re-investing in your business. Use this money to pay for equipment maintenance contracts, to buy supplies, for additional advertising, and for generally improving your business.

Now set aside an additional 5% for fun -- pure and simple fun! It's vital to your mental health. Without some fun, this business becomes as much of a drudge as your old job and can lead to health problems as well. When that happens, you've defeated one of the primary reasons for being self-employed. You're no longer in control, no longer happy at what you're doing.

According to a fact sheet recently released by the Women's Bureau of the U. S. Department of Labor, "it is frequently the woman's earnings which raise a family out of poverty." They also report that, "a majority of women work because of economic need." In 1988 almost two-thirds of the women in the labor force were single, widowed, divorced or separated, or if married, their husbands were earning less than $14,000 a year. The 1990 census figures may be even higher. With those facts and figures in mind, be sure you analyze your

budget carefully so you can set your income goals
according to your needs.

FOURTH, now that you've figured out how much money
you'll need, determine what resources you have to get
started? Do you have any available cash? any savings?
any assets to trade for what you need? a good credit
rating so you can buy equipment or arrange a lease?
This will be discussed more thoroughly in Chapter 4,
but start thinking about it now. Start listing all
your financial pluses and minuses so that when you
start planning your actual purchases, you'll know where
you stand.

FAMILY MATTERS

How supportive will your family be? Will they
understand and cooperate when you need uninterrupted
time to work? Will they complain that the typewriter
noise is interfering with their TV enjoyment? Will
they understand when you send out for hamburgers three
nights in a row while working on a deadline?

Will they help with housekeeping duties at all?
Will they take phone messages when you're out? If you
have small children, will you be able to afford a sitter, or will you have to wait to type until they are in
bed?

These will be the hardest questions to answer,
because you aren't the one who can answer them. Your
family might not be able to answer them, either,
because they don't know what to expect and can only
speculate as to how they will act and feel. In addition, they may be less than honest about their commitment to your new venture because they don't want to
hurt your feelings.

I'll be perfectly honest with you. This is the
part of the business I found the hardest. My husband
still has a little difficulty being known as "Peggy
Glenn's husband." He's also not very happy when I work
at night.

My kids resented it sometimes, too, especially
when a deadline interfered with their plans for my
involvement in their social life. (It was a different
story, though, when they wanted me to type a school
paper for them at 9:30 at night so they could take it
to school at 7:30 the next morning.)

I actually got more help with housework when I had my "real job." It was easier for my family to identify that I was "working" when I was out of the house. The way in which I solved my dilemma, at least temporarily, was to go on a strike. After I made my point, we had a calm discussion at which I pulled my best dictator act and announced that they had two choices:

(1) they could all help with chores on a proportional share basis (hubby included); or
(2) they could all chip in financially according to their individual ability to pay and we'd hire a housekeeper.

The vote was for option #2. As teenagers, the kids all had the ability to make a little money. This plan actually worked out rather well. In between the weekly housekeeper days, they were embarrassed to let things get too out of control, because they didn't want the housekeeper to see how careless they were. It was okay for Mom to scrub toothpaste out of the bathroom sink, but it was out of the question to have the housekeeper see how poor their aim was.

This arrangement was quite successful until the housekeeper moved to Kansas. We never hired another one, our oldest daughter moved into her own apartment, and I just resigned myself to having a "comfortable" house instead of a clean one.

When I first started talking about quitting my job and trying self-employment, my husband was very uneasy. He's one of the quiet cautious types, and he wasn't sure I could bring in enough money. At the time, we really depended on my income. We still depend on my income. I proved myself, but his hesitancy was difficult to accept when I was feeling so enthusiastic.

He was skeptical, and I think his skepticism just made me work all the harder to prove I could do it. I told him that I was certain I had a saleable service, especially since we live in an area with lots of colleges and universities. I was confident that I could generate more than enough steady business with some well-placed advertising.

Your family may have routines and customs that cannot be changed. If anyone in your family needs your attention for medical matters, be sure that you will have enough time to handle those tasks and still run a business, even a part-time one.

SPECIAL CIRCUMSTANCES

"Hotel, motel," visitors, recreation activities

If you live in a popular vacation area of the
country (mountains, beaches, amusement parks, etc.),
will visiting friends and relatives from out-of-town
pose a problem for you? How will they react when you
decline to participate in a day's activity because you
must finish a term paper, a financial report, a legal
brief, a doctor's dictation, or a writer's manuscript?

If you'd like to spend time with your guests, schedule
the time for a vacation, and arrange for another typist
to cover your customers. If, on the other hand, you'd
love an excuse to dodge spending time with your guests,
then type away. I'll never tell!

Handling your hostess duties and your business
duties will often require all the tact and diplomacy
you can muster. If you always treat your home-based
business seriously, I don't think you'll encounter too
many problems. No doubt, you'll have the opportunity
to balance business and hostess duties more easily than
if you had an 8 to 5'er, but don't lose sight of your
commitment to your customers and their deadlines.

The neighbors

And don't forget the neighbors, Very often, even
well-meaning neighbors will forget that you're really
in business. You may often be asked to be available
for babysitting chores, to chaperone repair workers, to
oversee delivery of furniture and/or parcels, to check
the roof in a rainstorm, or any one of a thousand
things that good neighbors do for each other, particularly if one of those neighbors just happens to stay in
the neighborhood all day. This doesn't mean that you
can't occasionally help out in an emergency, but make
sure you aren't taken for granted.

Physical disabilities

If you're physically disabled, do you need an assistant
to help you run your business? If you're unable to
travel freely, you might want to hire someone to help
with pickup and delivery to inaccessible buildings if
your specialty is commercial typing. If you're a
quadriplegic, you'll probably need an assistant to feed
the paper into the typewriter and remove it when you're
ready to work on the next page.

If you have any speech impairment -- cerebral palsy for instance -- you'll want to consider arranging for a person to help with telephone messages. If you're deaf, you may also need a message service or a telecommunications device specifically designed for your needs.

None of these disabilities should be seen as roadblocks, however. With the advice in this book, with a few assistive and/or adaptive devices and a few pieces of high-tech equipment, and with sound guidance from a vocational counselor, there is no reason a physically disabled person can't make good money with a typing business. An occupational therapist reminded me that quadriplegics have reached amazing speeds with a mouth stick or a forehead appliance. Determination and skill usually win out over adversity.

Family "roadblocks"

If you live with your parents, will they allow you to introduce a business activity into the home. Will they permit phone calls and visits from customers at irregular hours? If they don't seem very supportive of your plan for home-based self-employment and need extra convincing that you're not off on another hare-brained idea, try enlisting their help. This may get them off your back and on your team. Can you put in your own phone line? Will younger or older brothers or sisters interfere with your work?

Will the family be courteous to customers on the phone and at the door? Will they take messages when you are out? Can you say no to friends who want to socialize when you have a deadline to meet?

Childcare

If you have young children, I strongly recommend that you make arrangements for a sitter or child care. Even if you don't work while your youngster(s) visits the sitter or child care center, you'll enjoy the free time, if only for an hour every other day or so. I have talked with scores of mothers of young children about how they handle the dual roles of mother and businesswoman. One woman has a legal transcription service at home, several have medical or general typing businesses at home, many type for students, another sells Tupperware, and they all agree that a reliable babysitter or child care center is an absolute necessity.

I can't talk from experience about trying to run a home-based business with babies or toddlers at home, because my children were teenagers when I started my business. But all the women I've interviewed who have young children gave me the same answer -- it was unanimous -- hire a babysitter or use child care on a regular basis. The single mothers were more emphatic than the married ones. They all said they needed an occasional break from mothering duties.

Try to remember that although your children are a part of you and they're a part of your home, they aren't a big part of your business. Define their role early, and redefine it as they grow up and their needs change. Your family will be happier if the conflict and stress is kept to a minimum. This is the same as if you worked outside your home at another job.

> Is the goal so far away?
> Far, how far no tongue can say?
> Let us dream our dream today.
> -- Alfred Tennyson

SUMMARY

So now you have looked at the primary considerations before getting started. Actually, this self-examination is the first step in getting started. You've reviewed the whys and why-nots. You've looked at your personality, your financial situation, your family status and any special circumstances. Take a week or so to mull it all over in your mind; talk with your family, friends or relatives, or anyone who can give you support and be a good sounding board. Next, make a two-column list of your own "why" reasons and "why not" reasons. Make another list of your strengths and weaknesses. Make one more list of your overall goals -- for this month, for six months from now, for one year from now.

Recognize that you have limitations and admit to them. Try to point them out to your family, too. If you decide to work at home a d will be leaving a tradi-tional job outside your home, it's true that you may have a little more time for household responsibilities. You can type at the same time that the dishwasher or washer and dryer are running; you can type while the crockpot does its thing. But it's impossible to type and vacuum simultaneously, type and dust, or type and mop floors or fix an elaborate smorgasbord luncheon. On the other hand, if you've been at home and not working, expect that you will not accomplish as much in the home once you start working.

Look at it your way and make a decision based on your unique needs. I told you how I did it, but no other person's life is like mine. Pick and choose what works best for you. And don't approach this whole thing as if your very life depended upon making the perfect decision. All throughout your life, and certainly throughout your working career you'll be faced with decisions. The best you can do is to gather as much factual information as possible, evaluate all your data carefully, and make a decision that feels right to you without causing anyone else any hardship.

Sometimes you'll be an instant success, sometimes the new way will be a struggle and you'll get there eventually, and sometimes you'll be a complete flop! Whatever the outcome, the biggest mistake you can make is not even trying. The modern proverb goes something like this: "the only real failure is failing to try."

If you're really scared to leave a secure job, try the home typing business on a part-time basis while you still have your "real job." Ease into it slowly. You can do a small job now and then during non-working hours. For some customers, your availability at these times will be an asset.

If you haven't been working, you don't have as much to lose, but self-employment can be just as scary, if not more so, since you're re-entering the work world and don't know if it's a jungle or paradise. Starting to work again or for the first time won't be without its fears and frustrations. But once the business gets off to a start and the profits trickle in, it'll be worth it.

Trust me, you'll be pleasantly surprised to discover that some strong personality traits that may cause you all kinds of grief in a job, are perfect for self-employment. Again, using my information to illustrate, look at the comparison on the next page. I've often marveled at how what is accepted as natural and ordinary in a self-employment environment is completely foreign and forbidden in a traditional work environment. Again, there is that aspect of: are you the one who is BEING controlled or are you the one IN CONTROL?

21

This is the "BEFORE" and the "AFTER" Peggy Glenn in the eyes of former co-workers and present colleagues respectively.

BEFORE	AFTER
stubborn	determined, persistent
outspoken/critical	courage to stand up
conceited, brash	sure, confident
nosy	sharp, inquisitive
just a secretary	professional typist

I like the new list better than the old, and I'm still the same person. But now that I'm self-employed, my ways are acceptable. Before they were cause for friction. What will your two lists look like? Will you be pleased?

Ready to read on? Let's go! There's an ancient Chinese proverb that states, "A journey of a thousand miles starts with the first step." You don't have to go a thousand miles, you've already taken several giant steps, so how about a few more?

CHAPTER 3

Finding Your Customers: Five Major Markets

This book is intended for the person who has average or better typing skills; but don't be frightened away if you are a beginner or if your skills are rusty. If you have some time to invest and are willing to learn, you, too, can be successful at a home-based typing business.

THE BEGINNER

As a general rule, once you can type a single page of double-spaced, non-technical text with pica type and standard academic margins in 10 minutes (with no more than three errors), you are ready to hang out your shingle. This is the bare minimum. Although typing speed isn't extraordinarily critical for all typing jobs (sometimes you'll be given written or dictated work you can't read or understand), typing speed of at least 50 words-per-minute is the minimum industry standard. If you can't type that well, then be willing to spend a great deal of time learning to type and/or practicing what you learned many years ago.

How are you going to learn? Probably the best way is to enroll in a typing class through your public school system's adult education department or at a community college. In most cases these classes will be free or nearly free, and you will be able to use modern typewriters. In some areas, you can enroll in job-retraining centers to learn or brush up on typing and other office skills.

If you already know how to type but are extremely slow, then practice is what you need. Again, enrolling

in an intermediate typing class may be your best bet.
If you have a typewriter and can practice at home, do
it. Type letters to friends, retype stories from magazines and newspapers, type, type, type! Many public
libraries in large cities have coin-operated typewriters available. My librarian tells me that she
knows of no full-service library in the country that
doesn't have a typing instruction book, either.
Perhaps your typing skills are in fine shape, but
you're rusty about current practices, procedures, and
formats in the business world. Working for a temporary
agency will help you upgrade your skills and may also
help familiarize you with the current office machines.

You might also consider an excellent book:

BRUSHING UP ON YOUR CLERICAL SKILLS,
by Eve Steinberg. Arco Publishing

If you're reading up this book of mine, it's
evidence that you are seriously considering typing or
word processing at home. With just a little more determination, some time, faith in yourself, and acceptable
typing skills, you can do it. You really can!

THE EXPERIENCED WORKER

So, now, if you are an acceptable or better typist, how can you match your skills with a particular
market? Start by carefully looking (and listing again)
your skill assets. Is there any subject area in which
you have expertise: from prior employment, from volunteer work, from personal interests? Have you learned
any special terminology from your spouse, children,
friends, parents, or from a previous job?

Next, is there a need for your special skills
where you live? Will there be a demand for you and
your vocabulary or talents or special competencies? Be
sure you match the available work with your available
skills. A mis-match could be disaster. For instance,
if your background is agriculture, mining, or forestry,
you may not have much of a market in the middle of
Chicago. By the same token, you may not do well with
academic typing in an industrial area.

What extra do you have that will make you just one
notch above the competition? Do you have excellent
grammar and punctuation skills? (That alone will make
you a lifesaver in a nation that is increasingly

illiterate on paper.) Are you a competent editor and can you "fix up" reports, letters, proposals, and manuscripts?

Are you fluent in any language besides English? Can you take shorthand, and would you be willing to do it over the telephone? Do you have bookkeeping skills that you can combine with your typing skills to offer a more full-service program to your customers? Do you have additional "side" skills such as calligraphy, graphic arts ability, a notary's license or seal?

Using plain paper or a steno pad, make a list, such as the one below, of all your experience and side skills, whether you were paid for them or whether you acquired them by doing volunteer work.

-PAID -

-Store clerk - people skills
              handle money

-Secretary - trucking company

    bills of lading, customer
    contact, driver schedules,
    payroll, interstate commerce

Admin. Ass't - school district
        personnel, contracts, proposals,
        government reports

      - VOLUNTEER -
Scout leader - travel, meetings
Neighborhood Watch - speakers, programs,
        travel, newsletter, mailings

WHAT ARE THE MAJOR MARKET CATEGORIES

In my experience, there are basically five major markets for the home-based typist: academic, business or commercial, medical, legal, and professional writers. Within each of these areas, of course, are sub-specialties; and as I explore each of them, be thinking about your experience and where you can put it to use in the most pleasurable and profitable manner. Making money and having fun IS possible. Trust me.

ACADEMIC TYPING

This sort of typing covers everything from a 3-page book report for a high-school student to a textbook written by a university professor. In between are: term papers, essays, research reports, take-home exams, masters theses, doctoral dissertations, course outlines, grant proposals, resumes, and curriculum vitae.

In an academic typing business, you may not see all of these things, but you will certainly see a variety. The most valuable skills you can have in doing this form of work are attention to details and accurate spelling, punctuation, and grammar.

A strong editing ability will be an asset if you work for post-graduate students, for faculty members, or for adults who are returning to school to obtain an academic degree to supplement earlier vocational training. Today, many people who received vocational degrees to enter their chosen field (nurses, police officers, teachers), now find that they need an academic degree or an advanced academic degree to be promoted. (You know the new line, "I don't care how well you do your job, do you have a college degree?") If you have the ability to "translate" their occupational jargon into academically-acceptable language, you will never go hungry.

I feel that this is the most lucrative, most flexible, and most readily-available market for the home-based typist. A metropolitan or suburban area is very likely to contain a high percentage of people who attend classes at some level beyond high school.

Think for a minute of all of your neighbors, relatives, friends, and co-workers who are going to school. Then think of all the people who are in their classes.

Multiply that by the number of classes at their
schools. There's your market!

If you live in an area that is close to a college
or university, the possibilities are even better. Now
your market extends to the faculty and staff employees
of the institution as well. Many public colleges and
universities are sadly understaffed clerically because
of budget problems, so the faculty members are forced
to go elsewhere to get any professional-advancement or
personal work typed.

You may have some competition in this area from
the secretaries at the schools. But remember, you can
be available during the day when they're working. You
can take care of the rush job while they're busy. If
you are one of those secretaries, do as I did. Use
your experience to its best advantage by leaving the
confines of a "real job" and being available for the
customer who needs your expertise.

One word of caution for the moonlighting college
or university secretary: Be very careful that you
don't use your employer's time or materials for your
own business. First of all this is unethical. It may
also be a violation of your employment contract and
grounds for instant dismissal if a complaint is filed.
In addition, it may be viewed as conflict of interest
and result in a heavy fine and/or dismissal, especially
if you work for a governmental agency. Check your
employee handbook if you have any questions.

If you don't have academic experience, but feel
that you can learn to do the work, there are a variety
of style manuals you should become familiar with:

APA (AmPsycholAssoc)	-- Publication Manual
Campbell & Ballou	-- Form and Style: Theses, Reports, Term Papers
MLA (ModLangAssoc)	-- MLA Handbook for Writers of Research Papers, Theses, and Dissertations
Turabian	-- A Manual for Writers of Term Papers, Theses, and Dissertations

These paperback books can usually be found in any college or university bookstore. They are also available in large commercial bookstores (B. Dalton, Walden-books, etc.). Read through these manuals carefully and thoroughly. Once you are familiar with the rules and formats, you will save valuable time. After you work with them a short while, the styles become second nature.

Other professional groups have style manuals and publication handbooks which deal with specialized areas: geologists, anthropologists, biologists, physicists, chemists, engineers, computer specialists, etc. Ask your customer if there is any special manual or format you are supposed to follow. If he or she has a copy of the manual or instructions, ask to use the copy while you type the paper, and then buy your own.

If you'll be working for students at one college or university in particular, become familiar with any special requirements of that institution. Very often all post-graduate work (master and doctoral degrees) must conform to the institution's own special format rules. Become familiar with the person or committee at the campus who is responsible for reviewing all these papers, and obtain a copy of the manuscript preparation guidelines for your own use and information.

BUSINESS OR COMMERCIAL TYPING

With a little ingenuity, this business and commercial typing can be done successfully at home also. Many small businesses and professional offices are in need of extra secretarial support. They may not have the finances or the workload to justify a full-time position, but nearly all of them need some form of clerical help.

One very excellent business customer for the home-based typist is another person who is also working from home: consultants, sales people, small manufacturing operations, etc. The "cottage industry" explosion gets greater and greater each year that money gets tighter and commercial office space becomes more expensive. Conventions and professional meetings are another source of business work.

The possibilities are limitless in this wide-open business and commercial area. As just a few examples, you can type:

1. menus for small restaurants and coffee shops

2. correspondence, mailing lists, and brochures
    for social groups, civic groups, associa-
    tions, church groups, etc.

3. real estate listings or financing proposals
    for independent real estate salespeople or
    brokers

4. general office work for all small businesses

5. invoicing and collection duties for small
    shipping or manufacturing companies

6. any kind of correspondence at all for the
    general public (complaint letters, letters to
    explain misunderstandings, holiday letters,
    community or club newsletters)

7. job resumes and letters of introduction

8. consultants' reports or correspondence, rang-
    ing from a psychologist's report, or an envi-
    ronmental impact report (lovingly known as an
    EIR), to a management proposal, a financial
    report, or a feasibility study, and more.

Think of your experience. What have you done that
would lend itself well to another small business and
provide valuable clerical support to that small business? Have you worked for freight or trucking companies? Do you have a banking background? Do you know
the plumbing business inside and out? Real estate?
Insurance? Automobile sales and service?

I could fill up the rest of this book just asking
you questions. But instead, I'll let you have the fun.
Find out what you can offer the business world in your
locale that no one else is offering. Or how you can do
it better, more creatively.

*   *   *   *

I've heard of a few things just recently that show
some ingenuity.

One woman provides a secretary/message service for
traveling sales representatives. She has such clients
as: a salesman for medical supplies, a salesman for
printing press supplies and equipment, and a saleswoman

for sportswear. She takes messages for them, types letters to their customers, maintains their mailing lists, and helps prepare their periodic sales and marketing reports.

One of her clients is also president of a professional organization, so she prepares that association's newsletter every other month and maintains all the files, correspondence, membership lists, etc., for that association.

Another woman works exclusively for small property-investment companies. She types agreements and proposals for only five companies, but that keeps her comfortably busy. She offers quick service, checks all the math, provides pick-up and delivery at $2 a trip, and is ACCURATE! She told me that she once discovered a $22,000 error in an early draft of a proposal, pointed it out to the investment company before the proposal was presented to anyone else, which saved the company considerable embarrassment, and she received a $50 bonus and a dozen roses! Now, I grant you, $50 might not sound like much for discovering a $22,000 error, but the proposal was only two pages long and her bill was only $17. I think a $50 bonus on a $17 bill is something to be proud of!

Another woman has some writing background and has also worked for an advertising agency. She prepares a newsletter and mailing labels for a small neighborhood grocery store. The store is fighting to compete in the world of the large conglomerate chain markets, and the owner pays her well to help him put "polish" on his newsletter.

She says that the store owner is convinced that he can attribute his increased sales to her help with the newsletter. He says that his customers appreciate the personalized touch. She is part of that and feels good about it. That's one of those extras -- pride -- that is so often missing in a standard secretarial job.

*   *   *   *

With just these three very different examples, you can see how varied the possibilities are for you. The work is there, you just have to go after it and make every customer glad that you walked into his or her store, office, company, or group.

If you need any help brushing up on your skills at letter writing, preparing reports, setting up resumes, and any business correspondence, invest in a good secretarial handbook. For less than $10 all the information you will need will be right on your desk all the time. My long-time personal favorite is the Webster's Secretarial Handbook.

MEDICAL TYPING OR TRANSCRIPTION

This field is opening up more and more for the home-based typist. You can do such things as: filling out health insurance claim forms; transcribing medical reports; preparing case studies for doctors, surgeons, dentists, or orthodontists to present at their annual meetings; transcribing pathology reports for clinical laboratories; preparing consulting reports for neurologists, psychologists, surgeons, physical therapists, and helping medical/dental offices with overload work.

If you have any experience in the medical field, even if it isn't office experience, knowing the terminology will be invaluable. You can use that knowledge to set up a traditional medical typing service by applying the ideas I just presented, or you can use it in other ways. Because of my combined medical and academic background, I had two very interesting customers.

One man puts on continuing-education seminars for nurses and dentists. Four times a year he needs to have a course outline and a syllabus typed. Because so much of the language is medically technical and because it has to be approved by an education board, he brought it to me instead of to a general business typist. And because I don't enjoy routine correspondence and general business work, he <u>doesn't</u> bring that sort of work to me. He used two home-based typists, and we were all happy with the arrangement.

Another very fascinating job I did was to prepare a newsletter/journal for an association of histotechnologists (highly specialized lab technicians). The president of the association was a woman who had worked across the hall from me when I worked at the university's medical school. She remembered me and my business (and my reputation on the job) when it was her turn to put out the newsletter.

In addition to paying me for preparing the journal, I was encouraged to put a small ad in one issue.

That ad produced a dozen new customers, most of whom were working on their own post-graduate school projects. Before long, the word was spreading throughout that local chapter that I was THE typist who could be relied on to be on-time and accurate. Soon, those new customers were referring other people they worked with. See how things snowball? And me in Southern California without a shovel!

From the research I've done, and in my own experience, you have to prove yourself and your skills a little more in this area in order to get customers. A majority of medical and dental offices are justifiably reluctant to sub-contract work out of their office. Doing so to the wrong person could seriously violate the confidential doctor/patient relationship. You must reassure them that you are confidential, dependable, and accurate. Ask them to consider that having you do the work in the confines of your home (an extra plus here if you live alone) is no different -- and perhaps better -- than their hiring an employee to work in their own office. Once you get the work, you'll get more. Your reputation will spread quickly, so make sure it's spotless.

LEGAL TYPING OR TRANSCRIPTION

If you've acquired any legal experience you'll be marketable in a home-based typing business that specializes in legal documents or transcription. According to my research, this is one area in which you must have prior experience in order to be successful at it at home.

If you don't have the experience, the only alternative I have uncovered is to offer yourself as an apprentice at an established office in order to learn the forms, the terminology, and the method of preparation.

If you have solid experience, you should be able to do very well with a home-based business. A woman in Los Angeles types for two attorneys who just passed the bar. Neither of them can afford a full-time qualified legal secretary, nor do they have the workload to justify one. She has plenty of work, though, by working for the three of them. The three attorneys share a small office that is staffed by a receptionist, and the secretary works from home. Once a week she meets with them to go over any special problems or discuss deadlines. Occasionally she has a "rush" job, but she usually works at a leisurely pace that suits her own wishes. Because she has some limited bookkeeping experience, she does their customer billing as well. They appreciate her, and she is happy with the control she has over her own hours and working conditions.

Another possibility in this field is helping already-established law offices and legal typing services with overload. If you are good, many firms will be very glad to have high-quality reliable temporary help. If you have a lot of experience, you might also enjoy offering "set-up" services to new attorneys who are opening new practices. Organize their files, start their bookkeeping system, order their office equipment.

One more outlet for your talents is transcribing the notes of court reporters and deposition services. A good deal of this work is often done on weekends or in the evening hours which makes it an ideal second job for someone who is already working but needs to moonlight, or an ideal job for a single mother who must work while her youngsters sleep or play.

In most cases you will type from dictated notes. If, however, you can read the reporter's notes, you will make almost twice as much. A woman in Pittsburgh, Pennsylvania, reports that she makes over $20 an hour doing court transcription. You can work for individual reporters on a contractual basis, or you can work for a court reporting service.

Unfortunately, this isn't always the highest-paying work you'll find. In most areas of the country, reporters pay a pitiful 50¢ to 75¢ a page for transcribing from their dictated notes. The work must often be done overnight, for not usually much of a bonus. In addition, if you type from actual courtroom or deposition tapes, people's speech patterns make understanding some of the words almost impossible.

The only way to make acceptable money at court transcribing is to be VERY fast or to be able to read reporters' notes. If you can read their notes without their having to dictate -- that is, if you help them eliminate a time consuming step in the process -- the pay rate per page is at least double in most areas of the country. Even at double the rate, the pay is still low when compared to other forms of typing at home. There are a few consolations, however. Many reporters and/or court procedures specify that the transcribed pages be typed in 9-pitch (9 letters to an inch), and

many of the pages are only 24 or 25 lines long and
these lines may contain fewer than ten words.

TYPING FOR PROFESSIONAL WRITERS

The final major market for the home typist is the
large number of writers and poets in this country. Publishing trade magazines estimate that there are over
seven million people in the country who are trying to
break into print, either for the print medium or for
television, radio, or film. These can range from the
poet to the textbook writer, from the novelist to the
how-to or cookbook author, from a writer of radio ad
copy to a television writer or playwright or screen-
writer and everything in between. An audience that
large may account for the fact that WRITER'S MARKET was
the #1 best-selling non-fiction book in the U.S. in
1979 and continues to be a big seller year after year.

This kind of typing is probably the easiest to do.
There are very few rules to follow, and they rarely
change. The only ones I know of are:

1. Always double-space (unless an editor speci-
    fies triple-space). On the average, a page
    will have 26 or 27 lines. NEVER prepare a
    manuscript (other than recipes or poems)
    single-spaced, and don't use space-and-a-
    half, either.

2. Always keep a consistent margin on all four
    sides. (That helps to estimate word count
    which is important.) Generally-accepted mar-
    gins are LEFT, 1-1/2 inch; RIGHT, TOP,
    and BOTTOM, 1 inch.

3. Don't hyphenate words at the end of a line.
    Go to a new line instead. If a manuscript
    goes straight to a typesetter, most of them
    put in all hyphens as permanent rather than
    as optional. Correcting a typeset manuscript
    for unwanted hyphens is a giant pain in the
    neck, not to mention a waste of time and
    money.

4. Paper should be 20 lb. bond, mimeo or xero-
    graphic paper is fine. Some writers may pre-
    pare their manuscript on 16 lb. tissue-like
    paper, but an editor would never accept this.
    Cotton-content ("rag-content") paper is not

as important anymore with the advent of the
copy machine. But erasable paper is a
definite taboo! The very feature of this
paper that makes it attractive to a novice
typist, i.e., its ease of erasure, makes it a
nightmare to an editor. The ink smudges and
wipes off, and in addition, the high sheen
produces an unbearable glare under fluores-
cent lights.

5.   Pica type is almost universally preferred,
      and make sure you use a standard typeface.
      Fancy typefaces spell almost certain rejec-
      tion of the writer's manuscript.

6.   Paragraphs are indented five or six spaces
      according to author or publisher preference.
      If a manuscript contains any long indented
      paragraphs (long quotes or special inter-
      views) these are still double-spaced, but
      within indented margins which are honored
      even if the paragraph extends beyond the one
      page on which it began.

7.   Film and television scripts and play scripts
      follow a very precise and very different for-
      mat. If you're not familiar with the format,
      ask your client to bring you a sample.

    Writers are usually very precise individuals who
don't need spelling and grammar help. (Even if some do
need help, they prefer to have a typist copy their work
exactly, making no changes.) So, you may not use your
editing skills when working for writers.

    One caution -- from personal observation, and
strictly my own opinion, so please don't send me hate
letters -- some writers are very impressed with the
fact that they are writers, particularly novelists and
poets. They are in love with the cultural aura that
surrounds them. They consider themselves several cuts
above the plebian typist. If you encounter this atti-
tude and don't care for it, you WILL NOT change the
writer. Better to bend a little if you can, or, if you
can't, refer the writer to another typist who doesn't
mind being treated as a subordinate.

    In all fairness, many writers, especially the
seasoned professionals, recognize that a competent and
caring typist will make their writing work so much
easier and will ensure that the finished manuscript

reflects top-quality skill, for the writer and the typist. A writer-client who fits this mold is one you wish you could clone.

Another advantage to the home-based typist who does this kind of work is that distance from a customer is not always a problem. Very often a writer will send his or her rough manuscript material through the mail or via United Parcel Service (UPS). The typist uses the same method to return the finished copy to the writer. In this way, a home-based typist in a rural area can still make a good living by offering high-quality work with fast turn-around time at a reasonable price.

Another caution note: an attorney friend advises that you NEVER accept a personal check from an unknown by-mail client. Ask for cashier's checks or money orders. Once you have established an on-going business relationship with this long-distance client, then you may revert to personal checks. This policy should be clearly written out, and signed by both you and the client, before you begin work on a long-distance project. More on this subject in the chapter, "Customers."

SUMMARY

I've explored what I feel are the five major markets for the home-based typing business: academic, medical, business/commercial, legal, and professional writers. I believe that by combining your skills with the available market where you live, you can be successful and happy in your business.

When looking at your skills and the potential market, consider anything that is special about you -- anything that sets you apart from your neighbor or co-worker. And don't be discouraged by any circumstance, any situation, or any perceived lack of skill or availability. Look for lemonade in every bushel of lemons. For instance, if you are physically handicapped (or if a member of your family is), turn that disability into a desirability. Consider how valuable a deaf typist is to the millions of deaf customers who are unable to communicate with hearing typists.

As another example, a woman in a wheelchair can be invaluable as an editor to an able-bodied writer who is preparing an article for a handicapped magazine.

Retired teachers and librarians could be booked months in advance if they offered research assistance to graduate students. Consider how valuable that would be to a corporate manager who works 10-hour days and is trying to get a master's degree. He or she would much rather pay a competent researcher who would spend a day in the library doing research than to cram one more chore into an already overcrowded leisuretime schedule. How about combining tutoring and typing? How about teaching typing in your home?

*   *   *   *

Your skills are much more valuable than you might think. Match them with a market, or create a market for them. After all, we didn't need hula hoops until someone created them and sold them so effectively that we all "had to have one."

Limber up your fingers, limber up your brain, and design an effective marketing campaign based on a careful look at your skills, the area around you and what needs to be done, and how much time and money you have to chase down the market. Money, you say? Yes, that leads us logically to the next chapter in the saga. Consider how much money you'll need for living and taking care of monthly essentials; for providing yourself with "benefits" such as vacation, insurance, sick leave; for buying equipment, supplies, or paying rent; and for doing some advertising or marketing, by reading carefully through the next couple of chapters.

MONEY

*Money is a guarantee that we may have what we
want in the future. Though we need
nothing at the moment, it insures the
possibility of satisfying a new desire
when it arises.*

— ARISTOTLE, 340 B.C.

CHAPTER 4
Financial Considerations

Money can put all that soul-searching and careful market analysis that you did while reading the first few chapters right back to square one. IF YOU LET IT!

Consider, though, that you CAN begin a home-based typing business for as little as $100 dollars or you can spend as much as several thousand dollars.

By taking note of your available financial and market resources, knowing your credit limitations, allowing for your own "employee" benefits, establishing an appropriate pricing structure, and keeping accurate records, you should be able to stay proudly in black ink from year to year. Paying your taxes on time will keep you out of the grips of the law.

Keep these three words in mind as you look at your money situation: NOW, GO, GROW. How much money do you need right NOW? How much money do you need to GO from day to day and make a respectable living at it? How much money do you need to GROW later on?

GETTING STARTED

As I just said, you can start a home-based typing business with a very small investment. A rented type-writer, a ream of paper, a bottle of correction fluid, a pen or pencil, and a ruler are all you need for a beginning.

There's nothing wrong with a simple beginning. I had only $60 to gamble when I started. In all truth, I couldn't afford to lose even that much, but I "blew my wad" because I had faith in myself and faith in the market for my kind of typing.

My first job paid $19. The next one paid $64, and my third one paid $44, a total of $127 in the first two weeks. With just those three jobs, I had earned enough to pay back my savings account for the $50/month type-writer rental and $10 worth of supplies, and we had $67 left for groceries. That's not much, but it was a start, and in time the jobs rolled in more regularly and we ate better.

Many people prefer to start on a little bigger scale than I did. If you have enough cash, go ahead and purchase your equipment and supplies right at the beginning. Try not to go into debt on this venture.

I've included a couple of cost estimates: one for starting a simple business with the bare minimum of equipment and a very small cash outlay; and one for starting more elaborately with a full complement of equipment and supplies. Feel free to use these figures as estimates or comparisons as you make your preparations.

The amounts were accurate in Southern California just weeks before this book went to the printer. With inflation running rampant from month to month, forgive me if the figures differ when you read this or if the cost of living in your area is different.

BARE BUSINESS ESSENTIALS

Typewriter rental for one month plus deposit	$65.00
	40.00
Rent one extra element for scientific client	10.00
Ream of inexpensive paper	5.00
Bottle of correction fluid	1.50
Extra ribbon and lift-off tape	7.00
Pen, pencil, ruler, paper clips	3.00
TOTAL NEEDED	$131.50

ALL SET TO GO
Money on hand, no loans

Typewriter purchase - "Selectric" type	$1,100.00
self-correcting, dual pitch, 15-inch carriage, 2 elements	
Purchase 2 additional elements for steady clients (Italic, math)	46.00
One-year maintenance contract on machine	92.00
Chair - new	110.00
Desk - used at garage sale	70.00
Supplies at local stationers	325.00

    pens, ruler, pencils, stapler, staples, correction fluid, ream of paper, copy stand, tape, 3 x 5 cards, 3-hole punch, paper clips, letter opener, staple remover, box of 100 #10 envelopes, dozen ribbons and dozen lift-off tapes

Business cards	35.00
Reference books - some used, some new	137.50
Telephone installation and deposit	185.00
	————
TOTAL NEEDED	$2,100.50

Here's another approach. Prepare your own
budget/shopping list using these categories:

1.   What are the "MUST HAVES"?

2.   What are the "WOULD MAKE IT EASIER'S"?

3.   What are the "STREAMLINED, ALL SET'S"?

FINDING THE MONEY

One of the first places to look for the money is
your own budget, your own resources. If you were
forced to scrape up $200 in a hurry -- in 90 days, for
instance -- could you do it? Is it possible to hold a
garage sale, a patio sale, a yard sale? Is there anything hanging around that you could easily sell? Is
there any spending habit that could be eliminated for a
month or two until you save up $50 or so (could you
pack lunches instead of buying them out)?

At the risk of sounding a little flippant, if
your refrigerator broke and you needed $200 to fix it,
you'd probably find the money somehow. If you depended
on a car to get to work and it broke down, you'd probably find a way to get it fixed or you'd make substitute arrangements until you could gather the money
you needed. By the same token, if starting your business is crucial to your financial or emotional survival, you'll find a way. I know you will.

I also sense that by now you're thinking, "what
kind of clairvoyant (or busy-body) is this Peggy Glenn?
Who is she to tell me to scrimp and save and scrounge
together the money to get going if I don't have a ready
bank account?" Well, "I" am really at least 300-350
other people just like you from all walks of life and
all corners of this country. I have received hundreds
of letters telling me tales of struggle and coping, and
telling me success stories. I can't begin to answer
them all, but perhaps you can take comfort knowing that
you're not the only one who'll start this and struggle
at it and probably succeed just as hundreds of others.

Look to your own resources first. At the risk of
sounding preachy one more time, if you must borrow, do
it from a financial institution. I've been very lucky
myself with family (not so lucky with friends), but
I've heard hundreds of horror stories from struggling
entrepreneurs about broken friendships or strained

family relationships as a result of loan misunderstandings. I'm not saying it will never work, often it does, but borrowing money from friends or family can be disastrous. Remember these famous quotes:

> Neither a borrower nor a lender be;
> For loan oft loses both itself and friend;
> And borrowing dulls the edge of husbandry.
> Shakespeare, 1601

> The borrower is servant to the lender.
> Proverbs XXII, 350 B.C.

If you don't have all the cash, but are comfortable securing a personal or business loan based on the strength of your existing assets or income, your business plan, and marketing research, do so. Be sure, however, that you have a solid market to support your debt. If you have to worry about making lease or purchase payments for equipment each month in addition to meeting basic living expenses, you may soon find yourself frazzled and wondering why you ever started this crazy venture. That defeats the whole purpose of self-employment. Worry and frustration are what you wanted to leave behind, remember?

The major typewriter dealers have a variety of purchase plans available. You can rent, rent with an option to buy, lease, lease with an option to buy, buy on credit, or buy with cash. On the average, one month's rental for a commercial self-correcting typewriter is somewhere between $45 and $70 depending on where you live and how much demand there is for the machines. Total purchase price on a new machine of the self-correcting variety is right around $1075.

Some office-machine dealers hold their own credit contracts, while others sell the contracts to a lending agency or finance company. If you have a good relationship with your bank, talk to the lending officer of your branch to see if the bank can offer a better deal on financing. The same is true if you belong to a credit union. Compare interest rates when shopping for a loan.

Credit is becoming more and more difficult to obtain with each month. The money supply may ease up, but you can bet that bankers and finance companies will be very cautious about the loans they write. You will have to prove that you are a very good credit risk and that you have a solid marketing strategy for your

business if you are to convince anyone to loan you the
money. Your best bet may be to start with a rental and
then buy the machine outright once you have saved
enough.

One of the biggest roadblocks to obtaining a loan
to start a home-based typing business, or even an
office-based typing/secretarial business, is that there
are no census or industry research standards available
for what we do. Bankers know about restaurants, bowling alleys, gas stations, dentist offices, and print
shops. But who ever keeps records on how successful we
are, how much it costs us to set up and keep going? In
many places, folks will simply snicker and say, "Oh,
she's taking in typing. Isn't that nice."

A personal note here, a painful one, but one I had
to swallow anyway. Two years ago when I needed a short-
term business loan for expansion on a special project,
I visited my friendly banker. I carefully explained my
detailed plan, showed him orders already in hand, and
was greeted with a pleasant, "Sure, no problem, come
back next Tuesday and we'll have all the paperwork
ready." But when Tuesday came, and I was to deliver a
check to the printer that afternoon, the banker said so
sheepishly, "Oh, you do realize I need both you and
your husband to sign for this." I was furious! livid!
I'd been in business for over 7 years. This banker had
watched my business grow and grow. But, still, my kind
of business wasn't something he was familiar with,
there were few if any industry statistics to back me
up, money was tight, his superiors watched every loan
he authorized, and I was trapped.

Fortunately I summoned all the business diplomacy
and self-control I possessed, called my willing husband
for his signature, and I had the check 3 hours later.
Be aware this might happen to you, too. Was it discrim-
inatory? Probably. Could I have fought it? Probably.
And won? Probably not, and the delay at that time
would have cost me real money instead of business
pride. That was also no time or place to throw a tan-
trum: in a small branch in the section of town where
all the Chamber of Commerce leaders traded, at a time
when I was seriously considering applying for membership in the Chamber.

You may find yourself in the same predicament when
it comes time to justify a loan for a home-based typing
business. You may face snickers, you may face "You're
going to do **WHAT**! for **MONEY**?" I'm not saying it's

fair. I'm only saying it may happen. Be prepared for
it, swallow it if you can, get a loan for a "new wash-
ing machine" if you must, or get the loan somewhere
else if you can.

One possibility that did look somewhat promising
was the Small Business Administration's (SBA) mini-loan
program for women who want to start their own businesses. I'm not going to explain the program in depth,
because there are many, many places where you can find
out about it, and the rules change monthly. Call the
SBA's office nearest to you, or go to the library and
ask the reference librarian to help you find magazine
articles which discuss it thoroughly. Your library
might even have a copy of the SBA brochure which outlines the program in detail.

Again, as with getting a loan from a finance company or bank, you'll have to present a strong business
proposal in order to get approval for the money. The
biggest factor in your favor will be your enthusiasm
and a thorough business plan. The biggest factor
against you is that neither the SBA nor anyone else has
much faith in home-based businesses -- not yet.

BUSINESS PLAN

Never heard the term? Neither had I until a few
years ago. Basically, it's the words on paper of all
the thoughts that have been flying around in your head
about your plans for your business. And the words are
written in a logical format so that someone else who
reads your document, your plan, could understand what
you were going to do and how you were going to do it
and why you were going to do it. In a nutshell, here's
a basic outline for writing a business plan:

     Statement of purpose
     Summary of your goals and objectives
     Start-up plans
     Introduction - what is the business
     Your marketing plan - who and where is your market
     Your financial plan -- credit or existing assets
     Operations - how it will work
     Advertising and promotion plans
     What's the competition
     Who are you and what are your qualifications
     What is your personal financial situation
     What management assistance will you need or use
     Any supplemental information

BENEFITS

You can save your business from financial ruin in case of illness, injury, or disability by subscribing to some form of employee benefit program or preparing your own tailor-made program. As a self-employed businessperson, it's foolish to be without at least a bare minimum of health insurance coverage and disability insurance.

Depending on your family situation, you may not need a separate health insurance policy. If you are covered through your spouse's employer, if your "real job" offers it, if you are covered under your parents' policy, or if you already have some form of health insurance, you're probably sufficiently protected at least in the early stages of your business.

But disability insurance is another matter. Don't be without it. Consider your financial vulnerability if you became ill for an extended period of time or had an accident and were unable to work. What would happen if your assets were seized to pay for major hospital bills, or if you were unable to pay your debts because you didn't have some form of short-term or long-term disability or income-protection insurance.

Through contact with the American Business Women's Association (ABWA), I learned of Support Services Alliance (SSA), a Blue Cross-affiliated firm. SSA provides life, health, and disability insurance AT GROUP RATES to independent or self-employed persons and small businesses. When I last reviewed their literature, the monthly cost for health insurance for an individual was approximately $75.

Write to either or both organizations at:

American Business Women's Association
9100 Ward Parkway
P.O. Box 8728
Kansas City, MO 64114   (816)361-6621

Support Services Alliance, Inc. (SSA)
P.O. Box 130
Schoharie NY 12157   (800)892-8925

You may also find excellent group insurance plans available through your local Chamber of Commerce. Consider joining for a variety of reasons: exposure <u>for</u>

your business, exposure to other business ideas, opportunities to attend seminars and workshops, and much
more -- plus the extra benefit of a group insurance
plan. An independent insurance agent may also be able
to help you shop for an individual health-care plan and
disability-insurance plan. You may choose a plan that
allows you to visit your own physician, or you may
choose a health-maintenance organization (HMO) that has
pre-designated outpatient facilities and hospitals.

Private retirement plans (IRA, Keogh, etc.) are
also available to self-employed people. The business-
accounts officer at your bank should be able to advise
you of what is available in your area. In fact, IRA's
and Keogh's are available through a variety of sources.
A reputable accountant should have information to help
you decide what plan is best for you and how you can
work it in with your income.

The public library has reference material on this
subject, as does the federal government's consumer
information center in Colorado. For a catalog of their
publications, send a postcard to:

> Consumer Information Center
> Pueblo   CO 81009

SETTING PRICES

Charging fairly and adequately for your services
is an important part of your success strategy. AND,
setting your prices is probably one of the most difficult aspects of this whole business venture. For one
thing, you may find that after years and years of being
told what salary you would receive and never negotiat-
ing for anything else, you all of a sudden find it
extremely difficult and perhaps impossible to put a
value on the work you do. For so long you've felt
second-class and subordinate, and now you're in charge
and the headliner act, and where do you start?

EXERCISE #1

One of the best ways to arrive at a starting point
for setting your prices is to do this exercise:

First: What is the prevailing wage in your area
            for a mid-level secretary? For the sake
            of this exercise, let's use $9/hour.

Second: To that $9, add one-third, $3.

            This is your "benefits" cushion. All
            business experts these days advise that
            it costs an employer roughly an addi-
            tional one-third to provide benefits to
            employees.
            Now we're at $12/hour.

Third: Now add an additional one-fourth, $2.25.

            That is your "inflation and capital
            improvements" fund. This will allow you
            to weather slight increases in the price
            of your own supplies or utilities with-
            out raising your prices too often. It
            will also allow you to save money for
            buying additional equipment, "re-invest-
            ing in your business." Now we're at
            $14.25/hour.

    How does that $14 an hour seem? Too high? Too
low? Just about right? At least it's a starting point
for future negotiations and "figgerings." From this
initial exercise, decide upon your fair hourly wage.
Remember that you're in business to make money and
you're also in business to deliver quality service at a
fair price. Only your conscience and the going market
can help you determine that critical hourly wage. I
can't give you a standard formula that can be applied
uniformly all over the country other than to have you
use the exercise above or the one below.

                        EXERCISE #2

    This exercise involves adding your expenses and
your monthly income needs together, dividing them by
the number of hours you are able to work, and arriving
at a minimum hourly wage. First let's consider a
single woman with no children in a rented apartment who
will buy equipment with a loan.

First: Monthly house expenses $850
            (rent, utilities, food)

            Monthly equipment payment $100

            Monthly incidental expenses $250

            TOTAL $1,200

                            48

Second: Divided by available hours (120) $10/hr
           30 hrs/week x 4 weeks

     At $10 an hour, this woman will barely be able to
make her expenses and exist from day to day. There's
no room for any growth, any unexpected money demand,
any slow week. She must bring her hourly wage into
balance with those guidelines back on page 14 under
"Budget Matters." She may find herself at $14 an hour
just as in the previous example. She may occasionally
be able to spend more than 30 hours a week at the
business, but for the sake of this exercise I also
decided that she was retired, with a slight disability,
and able to work about three-quarter time.

     Next consider a married woman with a toddler and a
second-grader who plans to spend 20 hours/week on her
business; a half-time operation will fit in perfectly
with her family's schedule, and after working full-time
for a few years, she wants a break. Further suppose
that she needs $1,100 a month to meet her share of the
household expenses and make the loan payment on her
equipment. Divide the $1,100 by an average of 80 hours
a month and she arrives at $13.75/hour.

     Have you followed the procedure so far? Using
these two exercises, or a modification of one of them,
or a combination of both of them, do your own figuring
to arrive at an hourly wage. Then it's on to the next
step in the procedure.

     No matter how you price the work you do -- by the
line, by the page, by the hour, by the document, or by
keyboard time -- make sure you don't make less than
your pre-determined hourly wage. For instance, if you
figure that from handwritten copy you can type seven
pages of academic manuscript in an hour (time to proofread, too), the "average price per page" for academic
typing would be $2. Caution: read pages 50 & 51 about
that "page" and when you must deviate from that per-
page rate in fairness to you and your customer.

     Another method is to determine the current price
structure where you live and will be setting up your
business; then set your own prices accordingly. Be
aware, that "going rate" will be different everywhere.
For instance, the rate for typing in Huntington Beach,
CA, is probably lower than the rate for New York City,
and higher than the rate for Pittsburgh or Boise.

Also consider the going wage for secretarial employees in your area. A study by the Administrative Management Society showed 1989 secretarial salaries to range from a low of $286/week in some industries/areas to a high of $762/week in other industries/areas. In your specialty, in your location, what's fair?

One strategy that might give you an idea of the going rate in your area is to call every typing and secretarial service listed in your Yellow Pages. Call the ones with offices, and the ones that operate out of homes. Unfortunately, because too many people are afraid of competition, you may have to be just a little devious. I don't like to do it this way, and I don't like to suggest that you do it this way, but regrettably sometimes there is no other way. When you call these other services, pretend you have a manuscript that needs to be typed or pretend you have a series of business letters with envelopes. Ask how much it will cost and how soon the job can be completed.

Then take the highest per/hour or per/page estimate and compare it with the lowest estimate. As a starting point, you might consider setting your prices right in the middle. For example, if Fox Business Services charges $22/hour, $4/page, and 15¢/line; and Pat Jackson on Elm Street charges $6/hour, $2/page, and 7¢/line; then you might be comfortable setting your prices at $14/hour, $3/page, and 11¢/line. By being right in the middle, you may acquire the customers who are "sitting on the fence" for either of the other prices.

In my personal opinion and based on my experience in metropolitan or suburban areas, no typing job is worth less than $6/hour, $1/page, or 9¢/pica line. By the same token, I think it's a little presumptuous to charge more than $35/hour, $10/page, or 25¢/pica line. I realize that there are all kinds of function or location factors that may make that previous statement seem ridiculous (either too high or too low), but that's my personal opinion after being in business for more than 5 years and after talking to or corresponding with at least 2000 people nationwide.

Naturally, these rates are based on working from copy that is legible, understandable, and non-technical. Doing scientific, technical, and columnar work is much different and demands a significantly higher level of concentration and skill from the typist and therefore a much higher price. In addition, taking dictation from or transcribing tapes for someone who mumbles or speaks with an accent or has volume changes in his or her voice would also demand a higher wage.

There are reasons for charging sometimes by the hour, sometimes by the page, and other times by the line. There are also reasons for deviating from your standard pricing structure. Let's consider a couple of examples:

EXAMPLE 1:

A college research paper will probably consist of: a title page, table of contents, double-spaced text, a chart or table of some kind, footnotes and a bibliography. Each one of those pages has a different format to it. Each takes a different amount of time to type. Therefore, charging by the page may not work out fairly to the typist or the customer. In this case, an hourly rate is much more reasonable.

If another college paper is a lengthy essay with no references, no charts, and no title page, it will be more fair to charge by the page -- especially if you are typing from already-typed copy. If you are typing from handwritten copy, it's a matter of judgment. Is the handwriting as easy to read as typed copy? If not, if it's so difficult to read that you have to slow down to type from it, then forget the per/page rate and charge by the hour. This is an example of why sometimes it doesn't matter if you type 50 words-per-minute or 100 words-per-minute. If you can't read the job, you can't type it very fast.

EXAMPLE 2:

A business letter with accompanying financial proposal is a standard package for many firms. The letter doesn't generally pose a typing problem (unless you have to correct grammar and spelling). But a 4-page financial proposal of tabular presentations or mathematical computations may take several hours to complete. If you charged $1.25/page or even $2.00/page for a job like that and it took you 3 hours to complete, you'd be robbing yourself! In this case, an hourly rate is definitely more appropriate.

In other instances a per/line charge is more equitable. Firms that complete medical insurance claim forms often bill by the line. Medical transcription is the most common area in which this pricing method is

used. If medical reports, pathological reports, or
case histories are dictated and then transcribed onto a
plain sheet of paper, the line rate works out better
for the typist.

When bidding on a transcription job like this, or
when quoting a rate on this sort of work, keep in mind
that every person's method of dictation is different;
some talk fast, some slow. Some customers or firms
prefer pica type, while others prefer elite. Listen to
the dictated tape, and ask specific questions about the
finished requirements of the job before you quote a
price. More on this issue in Chapter 8, "Customer
Relations."

In legal typing or transcribing, the pricing
method seems to vary. Some charge by the line, others
by the page, others by the hour, and still others by
the document. Because of the wide differences in the
sort of work that is done, my best advice again (don't
I sound like a broken record by now?) is to call around
and see what the going rate is. Then set your prices
at a comfortable point for a beginning and raise them
when you get a steady supply of clients or when you
feel your skills or equipment demand a higher fee.

*   *   *   *

Also consider adding surcharges for pickup and
delivery, "rush" work or work that must be done on weekends, corrections, illegible handwriting, illegibly
marked-up typewritten copy, copy that arrives on scraps
of paper or written on both sides of the page, tapes
that are nearly impossible to understand, directions
that are unclear or contradictory, unnecessary interruptions, "after hours" appointments, unannounced
visits, etc.

As I said at the very beginning of this section,
setting your prices will be difficult, and I don't mean
to sound evasive on the subject. It's just that there
are no hard-and-fast rules or formulas for doing it.
Remember to first make the mental switch into an "if
they could do it themselves, they wouldn't be hiring
me", and an "I'm good" mode. Remember also to keep in
mind your minimum hourly wage requirements and your
monthly income requirements. Last, but not least,
check out your competition and the prevailing wage for
a good-to-excellent secretary and set your prices somewhere in the middle based on your skills, your
expenses, and the kind of work you plan to do.

As an overall pricing philosophy, if you charge too little you won't earn enough money to pay your bills and you will probably attract a less desirable group of customers. If you charge too much, you will scare many of the customers away. Pick a spot in the middle of the road and then move to the left (the faster traffic) or to the right (the slower traffic) when necessary. Please always remember, though, that it's not a crime to earn a decent wage for good work.

You can afford to undercut your competition a little bit in the beginning to gain a stable source of customers. But don't be a bargain! Bargain rates attract only bargain customers with bargain-quality work that is often boring and unpleasant.

GETTING A RAISE

Raising your prices can, and should, be done gradually as you become more skilled at what you do, to keep pace with rising costs, and particularly if you begin to do more and more complex assignments for your steady customers. Good business sense dictates that you re-examine your operating budget every six months or at least every year. Is your income keeping pace with your outgo? Are you making a profit or merely scratching out a living? Do you feel as if you're working more and more hours and bringing in less and less money proportionately?

If you upgrade your equipment, your prices will need to reflect the increased sophistication in both your equipment and your skills. It's entirely possible that you'll lose a few customers in this process, but perhaps as you grow or as you change, you'll find that you enjoy one particular kind of work and customer better than another. This is one more reason why you need that back-up network of other typists that I discussed earlier. You can refer out the customers that you've outgrown, yet you can be secure in the knowledge that these customers will still have their business needs met professionally.

Other customers will stay, partly because their business has changed as yours has, and partly out of loyalty. That's one of the most wonderful features of doing business in America. Everyone is free to choose, and loyalty is okay. It's kind of like being fond of a particular brand of spaghetti sauce or coffee or shoes. If that's the one you like, you stick with it even if it costs a little more, because you are always sure of the quality and because you "just plain like it."

In order to raise your prices, however, you have to feel as if you're worth it. I received a call just recently from a woman who said, "Every time I tell a customer how much I charge, I feel so guilty. I could NEVER raise my prices." Working for the love of it will never buy peanut butter and jelly or bacon and eggs, or pay the rent or turn on the electricity. At the risk of preaching one more time, you're worth it or someone wouldn't be hiring you to do it.

Getting a raise this way -- as the owner of the firm -- is less painful than asking the boss or going through a bureaucratic merit-increase evaluation process. If the market will bear it, charge more. If your equipment is more sophisticated, charge for its use accordingly. No strikes, no working without a contract, no hard feelings after collective bargaining or threatening to quit. Simple! Now back to work!

KEEPING RECORDS

Record-keeping is essential if you are to have any reliable measure of your business's growth and stability. This aspect of being in business is very unpleasant for me. I'm much happier just doing the work and leaving the business details alone. I have all I can do to manage a checkbook for my personal bills -- never mind a separate one for my business. But it has to be done, so if you're like me at all, do it in the easiest and least painful way.

For those of you with bookkeeping and accounting experience, this won't be a problem. But bear with me and my friends who are word experts, not numbers experts.

The basic steps are:

(1) keep track of all the income from the business

(2) keep track of all business-related expenses or money taken out as earnings.

Sounds simple, doesn't it? How much money comes in, how much money goes out, and why, what, where, when. It really is simple, but I still put it off as long as

I can every month. I manage to make a bank deposit once a week, and I manage to pay the bills twice a month, but beyond that, I'm not only lost, but I also border on being grossly incompetent by traditionally-accepted accounting standards. I'm not entirely comfortable with this lack of business knowledge, either. It's a little scary running a business and being so uninformed about good fiscal practices. As soon as I find some time, I want to take a short class.

I've hired a bookkeeping service, yet I still put off reconciling my actual receipts to the checks I've written until just about an hour before the bookkeeper arrives. Fortunately, once I've given her the receipts and she puts them into her computer, I receive a monthly print-out of just what money came from where, what money was spent for what, and how much is left for me or how much of a deficit I ran for the month. Of course, carry-over balances are what allow me to spend more in one month than I earned.

For business projection purposes, I keep a running notebook of my income on a very simple form. I plot this like a simple line graph so I can plan year to year what months will be flush and what months will need help from the previous or next month. On the same graph, I run a separate line (either with another color of ink or with a dotted line) to show the month-by-month expenses as compared with income. By plotting expenses this way, planning an equipment or supplies budget for the next year is a snap.

I also keep a simple log sheet on each customer. On that sheet I record the date of service, the general description of the job, the amount of the bill, and any special comments. When a customer fails to return in 3 months, I send a short note thanking her or him for the business, wishing them well, and reminding them of my hours and any new features. If they don't reply or bring more work within a month, I move the log sheet to the "Inactive" file. Performing this simple chore keeps me up to date on what months were good, what customers were the most regular, and how much they paid me.

That little tidbit probably belongs in the chapter "Customers," but since it also relates to projecting my cash flow, I put it in here because I thought of it first here. That information, like other pieces of advice and/or information in this book, has more than one application. Are you taking notes?

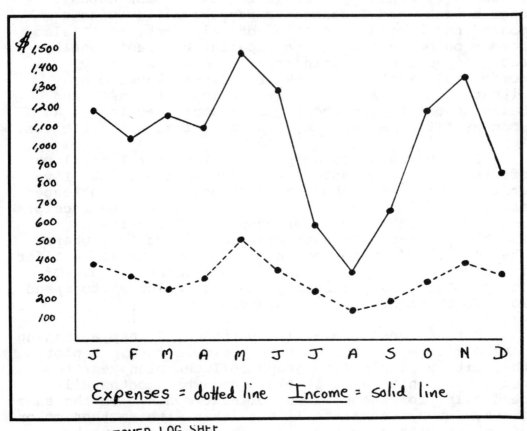

$ 1,500
1,400
1,300
1,200
1,100
1,000
900
800
700
600
500
400
300
200
100

J F M A M J J A S O N D

<u>Expenses</u> = dotted line   <u>Income</u> = solid line

CUSTOMER LOG SHEET

DATE   JOB DESCRIPTION DATE

Abby Hend

1/8	Eng. Report
1/20	History of
2/8	Resume
4/10	Intro le
	& Env
6/5	Disserta
9/20	Intro
	&
10/3	Movir

CUSTOMER LOG SHEET

JOB DESCRIPTION

John Burke   AMOUNT

2/6	Statements	
2/10	E.I.R. (river)	27.50
2/15	E.I.R. (Stone)	85.—
2/18	E.I.R. (White)	85.—
3/27	Consult (Jeffes)	93.—
4/6	Statements	183.—
6/2	E.I.R. (river 2)	27.50
		106.—

56

To keep track of expenses, I have a small petty-cash fund that I use for photocopies and incidental expenses, and I use my checkbook for all the rest of the bills. In order to keep the petty cash money separate from my personal money, I bought one of those small coin purses in the dime store (which now sells almost nothing for less than a dollar).

I save every single receipt. I have an expandable file folder which has enough pockets for each month. I match petty-cash receipts with the checks I wrote, and I note the check number on all other receipts. This helps me do month-end reconciliation before handing the paperwork to my bookkeeper.

Now, for those of you with more knowledge of this whole business than I have, keeping your own books is made easy by the availability of several excellent and well-explained record-keeping systems. The 2 systems I am most familiar with are: **Ideal** and **Dome**. Either or both of these systems will be available in your nearest office supply store or stationers. K-Mart carries one or both of them, also.

For learning the philosophy behind sound record-keeping as well as learning the basic steps for carrying out that philosophy, the best book I have ever found for managing the financial aspect of a small business is:

SMALL TIME OPERATOR, by Bernard Kamaroff, CPA
Published by Bell Springs Publishing.

The book's subtitle says it all, "How to Start Your Own Small Business, Keep your Books, Pay Your Taxes, and Stay Out of Trouble!" The book is easy to understand, clearly written, sprinkled with humor and candor, useful, factual, and gives more expert advice than I could ever hope to transmit in the small section of my book that you're reading now. I'm not in the business of selling other people's books, but this one is an absolute must if you're going to operate your business legitimately.

TAXES

This is the part of being in business that I loathe, detest, and positively hate. It makes me "mad as hell" (to quote Howard Jarvis) to give some of my hard-earned money to the government. But I have to if

I want to stay out of jail. (I've heard they don't have waterbeds, crisp celery sticks, or cable TV there.)

So file them I do. The paperwork process is relatively easy for me because I have a working spouse who has taxes deducted from his paycheck regularly. I am able to file my business taxes at the same time that we file the annual personal federal and state income taxes -- the April 15th variety. My business also operates on the traditional calendar year rather than on a different fiscal year (like the government which goes from October 1 to September 30). Even if you start your business in May, you may still consider your "business" year as January 1 to December 31, with five-plus months of operation in your first "year."

Each of you will have a different tax situation. The single woman with no other job may very well have to file quarterly statements of income as a self-employed person. Depending on your income projections and your earnings, you may or may not have to send a check with each quarter's filing. This is your way (courtesy of government regulations) of having taxes "deducted" from your "paycheck" which will satisfy your year-end tax liability.

On the other hand, suppose you're a single woman who types on the side -- in addition to a "regular" job where your employer deducts from your wages. In this case, your tax liability may be satisfied through those deductions from your "regular" paycheck. Perhaps you'll want to claim one less exemption just in case.

Also, because each of you will choose to operate your business differently -- some claiming every penny you earn, some claiming only the checks and pocketing the cash, and some claiming nothing -- no advice I could give would fit every one of you. I know that the "underground" economy exists. I know there are folks who type part-time to supplement meager pensions or Social Security incomes. I know that many, if not most, of these people do not report that income. I won't debate the rights and wrongs of this practice. If this is your way, YOU are the only one who needs to justify your actions to yourself and to any law agencies. I feel that it's completely out of my area to advise you about your taxes -- other than to tell you what you are supposed to do. I'm a typist, not an accountant or an IRS agent. I believe that being a professional in one field is sufficient.

My personal suggestion is to: (1) keep track of all income and expenses, (2) report all income and expenses, and (3) have your taxes done professionally by an accounting expert who knows the tax laws.

If you have any questions regarding the correct way for you to deal with the tax dilemma, consult an accountant for advice. The $25 or $30 you may spend for a consultation could save you from a hefty fine or penalty assessment from the IRS or state taxing agency (if you live in a state which collects personal income tax).

I had an accountant for my income taxes even before I started my business. Now at the end of the year I just give my bookkeeper's printouts to the accountant and she fills in all the blanks on the 1040 form and the Schedule C with the right numbers to keep the IRS authorities off my back. She depends on me to provide her with accurate information, and I depend on her to know the IRS laws regarding what I'm entitled to for deductions, depreciation, etc. We have a good bargain and we trust one another. (We both stay out of jail that way, too.)

TAX BENEFITS/DEDUCTIONS

Yes, there is a tax advantage to working at home, to running a business from your home, and in having legitimate expenses to offset income at the end of the year. Certain expenses that you could never claim if you had a "real" job, are routine deductions if you operate a business at home. For instance, you may legally deduct that portion of the mortgage (or rent), utilities, insurance, and maintenance that directly corresponds to the amount of square feet in your home which is used exclusively for the business. If you live in a home that is 1,200 square feet, and you use 120 square feet for the business (roughly a spot 4 feet by 3 feet), you can deduct one-tenth of all normal household expenses as I just discussed.

Any auto expenses that are directly related to running the business are also legitimate tax deductions. Keep a mileage log in your car and record all mileage that is business-related. At the end of the year, if you drove 25% of the miles for business and 75% for pleasure, then one-fourth of your auto expenses (payments, insurance, gas, oil, repairs) would be legal business deductions.

The biggest advantages to **starting** the business at home, even if you choose later to open an office away from home, are:

1. you save overhead expenses while you build up your business, and

2. you are also able to deduct some of your basic living expenses.

It's entirely possible that even though your business provides you with a living, that you'll have a net loss (a paper loss) at the end of the year and be able to receive a tax refund.

For instance, let's suppose that after paying all your direct out-of-pocket business bills, your balance sheet at the end of the year shows a $4,000 profit. That's income. That's taxable. However, using the example discussed earlier (one-tenth of the area of a 1,200 sq. ft. home or apartment), you may deduct one-tenth of the rent. Let's assume $500/month for 12 months for a total of $6,000 and your legitimate business tax deduction is $600. Then you may also deduct one-tenth of the utilities, let's assume another $200 for the year. Total deduction from that $4,000 now is $800. Last, you had $500 in auto expenses that you can directly charge to the business. So your deduction from that original $4,000 of taxable income is $1,300 leaving you with a NET gain of $2,700.

You earned the money, you spent the money, yet you gain the benefit of an additional $1,300 deduction which may reduce your taxable income to a point where you don't have to pay taxes on it at all or at least you don't have to pay as much. I realize that's a very elementary and simplified explanation, but you get the idea, I'm sure.

Again, read the information in Kamaroff's book, seek advice and counsel from a qualified accountant, and read literature provided by the IRS. Take what you're entitled to, but don't get greedy. You'll get caught and it could be expensive, not to mention embarrassing.

Two more tiny tidbits that I've picked up from one lecture or another, one book or another:

1. If it isn't a deduction, don't buy it or spend the money for it.

2.   Think tax benefits all the time. Read the
     business news all the time, attend seminars
     and workshops to learn more.

SUMMARY

I never said how much you can expect to make in a
week, a month, or a year. That figure is as variable
as there are people in the country who will be typing.
Some folks will leisurely type for 10-15 hours a month,
others will put in six 10-hour days a week. As a guess-
timate, I would say that for a part-time business you
can expect to bring in anywhere from $10 to $500 a
month; and for a full-time business, you can expect to
bring in anywhere from $10 to $2300 a month.

The variable factors are: what kind of work you
do, the simple term papers, or technical corporate
reports, or translating/editing; what the economy is
like in your area; how well you advertise; how many
hours you want to work; how you set your prices; what
your expenses are; and how well you stick to your budget.

Those income goals I discussed in Chapter 2 under
"Budget Matters" will be a big determining factor in
setting your prices and in deciding how many hours you
must work. On the one hand, if you need only $200 a
month for extra money, you can afford to work less than
half-time and charge moderately for your skills --
UNLESS you borrowed money to get your equipment and
supplies. In that case, you need to make enough money
to earn the $200 PLUS the payment on a loan.

On the other hand, if you are setting up the
typing business to replace your full-time job, you are
probably anticipating bringing in anywhere from $500-
$1,000 a month clear profit depending, again, on your
expenses. If you were earning $900, bringing home
$600, but spending $250 on child care and other work-
related expenses, you must now earn about $400 to break
even and maintain that 25% cushion.

Once your business gets rolling, there is no
reason you can't earn that $400 a month with a home-
based typing business. You'll probably find that you
don't need to spend 8 hours a day doing it, either.

If your business is highly specialized or technical, you can expect to command high prices while still

working less than a 40-hour week. If you're good at what you do, you'll be making well over $1,000 a month on a regular basis.

But the controlling factor is YOU. Not me, not your family, not even your customers. YOU have to be the guiding force in the business. You have all those fancy titles I talked about on page 8, remember? Put one on and sell your business.

My first two weeks were lean, and I've had lean periods every now and then over the years. But I stepped up my advertising, raised my prices a little bit at a time, and soon alleviated the problem. I started out with a rented typewriter, a package of paper, and a pencil, pen, & ruler. The first two weeks I worked on the kitchen table, and we either moved the typewriter to have meals or we ate on TV trays.

I continued to rent a typewriter for about 5 months. During that time, any repairs were the rental company's responsibility. At the end of 5 months, I had saved enough money to pay cash for the machine. My first month's rental fee was applied to the purchase price. When I bought the machine I signed up for a year's maintenance contract ($52) which guaranteed me unlimited service calls and parts. I feel that the $1/week was more than reasonable.

I'm sure that a maintenance agreement costs more than that now, but the expense is still justifiable. In a small one-person business, your business must function perfectly ALL the time. Good service for your equipment is absolutely mandatory. You can't afford to be down when a customer is on a deadline for the work he or she has entrusted to you.

I now own everything connected with my business. As it grew, I used that re-investment money talked about earlier and added a few items to suit my individual preferences and my customers' needs. I have a small calculator, a three-hole punch for students' papers, a ready supply of report covers, a light over the typewriter, a filing cabinet, office furniture, some specialized small equipment, etc.

By looking over my past records, I can anticipate which times of the year will be slow. I put aside money for those times, and I schedule vacations during them as well. One summer I took a whole month off! What job do you know of where you can get a month off after 3 years of working part-time? I consider my business a success for that reason alone.

I'm confident you can make your business successful, too. But you have to be willing to work at it, and you have to follow sound financial practices. Once your earnings are stable, all this money business will be easy and you'll be amazed at how well it all falls into place.

If you allow for some insurance, follow the business budget guidelines discussed in Chapter 2, set your prices carefully, adjust your prices when necessary, keep accurate records, and pay your taxes, you won't have money headaches. Don't be afraid to pick the brains of the money experts if you get into a temporary bind. Use the resources of an accountant, a commercial banking officer, other women in business, and the reference librarian if you have questions.

Now that you've considered all the "nuts and bolts" aspects of starting a home-based typing business, start writing a shopping list. The next section discusses what you'll need in the way of equipment, space, and supplies.

TAX - A compulsory payment
for which no specific
benefit is received in
return.

— U.S. TREASURY

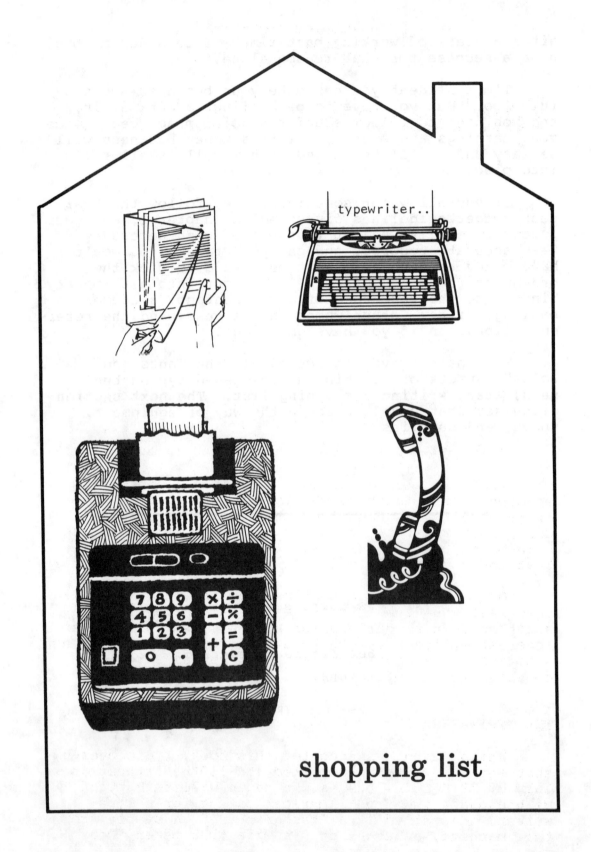

typewriter..

shopping list

CHAPTER 5
The Equipment You'll Need

You will need professional-quality equipment and supplies to do a professional-quality typing job. I want to discourage any of you from trying to start a typing business with a portable typewriter and some erasable paper. You can earn a decent amount of money with this business, although it isn't a get-rich-quick sure thing. Have you seen ads like these below?

"Housewives! Type while the kiddies are in school. Hundreds weekly possible with a little time and a typewriter."

"Homemakers! Make money with a portable typewriter and a little spare time."

I see red every time I read a paragraph in a book or see an advertisement that screams at you with such half-truths. People (or ads) like that, who prey on unsuspecting homemakers who desperately need to make extra money, are deceptive, unfair, and definitely don't know the first thing about how to run a lasting home-based typing business. Is there little wonder that the home-based typist is held in such low regard?

Oh, you may get a customer now and then who will take what you have to offer with your portable, but you won't be able to build a thriving business without at least an office-strength typewriter and a few tools and supplies to set you apart and mark you as a serious, conscientious professional.

THE TYPEWRITER...

While doing research for this book, I discovered that the typewriter celebrated its 160th birthday in July of 1989. In 1829, a man named William Burt of Michigan got the first American patent for a typewriter. He called it a "typographer." A sample from that machine, a letter to his wife that began "Dear

Companion," is on display at the Smithsonian National Museum of History and Technology.

That early machine was very slow and cumbersome. It consisted of a rectangular wooden box with typebars that faced downward around a circle. The "typist" rotated a lever to a position above the desired letter then pushed the lever to create an inked impression on paper. Today's label-makers are a similar adaptation of Burt's original design.

The typewriter as we know it today (at least the keyboard layout) was created in 1873 by Christopher Sholes of Milwaukee. Sholes was the 52nd person to "invent" the typewriter according to **THE WONDERFUL WRITING MACHINE**, a marvelous book by Bruce Bliven. It's worth an afternoon or two of reading. Try to find the book in your public library. I don't believe it's currently in print or available in bookstores.

When Sholes first designed the typewriter keyboard, he put the letters in alphabetical order, but this produced jamming -- especially of the D and E and the N and O which are frequently used together. There has been a lot of speculation and historical theorizing about how Sholes came up with the present keyboard arrangement. The explanation I like best is that he put all the letters of "typewriter" in the top row so that his salesman could demonstrate the machine easily. After he spread the rest of the letters out in random form, he added Q, U, and O to the top row to make the three rows of letters almost equal.

Few inventions have had as large an impact on our lifestyle as the typewriter. And the machine as we know it today has come a long way from the original relic. With the advances in electronics and telecommunications, there is no end to the technology and improvements in a simple keyboard and letter-printing machine. My using a word processor to simulate a typewriter in this book is but one very simple example. I have visions of some scientist working in a laboratory making modifications to our communications technology as I write this.

Remington and International Business Machines (IBM) were the leading manufacturers and innovators in both manual and electric models during the early part of this century. IBM still leads the field in office machine sales as indicated by sales figures in almanacs, sales periodicals, and other reference material

my friendly librarian found for me. A quick survey of
an office machine catalog, however, shows several manufacturers working hard to catch up. Many offer inno-
vations, many offer lower prices, many offer extra
features.

Other typewriters available in this country
include Smith-Corona, Royal, Silver-Reed, Exxon, Casio,
Olympia, and Olivetti, Brother, Canon, Facit, Exxon,
Panasonic, Toshiba, Xerox, not to mention private
labels for the major department stores.

The typewriter has been combined with accounting
and computer technology to produce bookkeeping
machines, and data-entry systems. For the purposes of
this book, however, let's talk about what you need for
your business. I think Mr. Burt and Mr. Sholes would
be proud of you and me and our entrepreneurial spirit
while using his noteworthy invention.

I've already stated emphatically that you need an
office-strength machine. I hope you believe me. A
typewriter should have the following features:

dual pica/elite capability

interchangeable type styles

variable vertical spacing
(single-space, double-space, space-and-a-half)

a correcting mechanism

easily-changed ribbons and correction tapes

and a 15-inch wide carriage.

Several companies make machines which have all or
most of these features. My research indicates that
electric typewriters equal to the IBM Correcting
Selectric   cost right around $1,000. Electronic type-
writers that are equal to or better than this industry
standard are comparable in price.

One bargain these days is the used IBM Correcting
Selectric. Many businesses and offices that have converted to computers and word processors have sold all
their electric typewriters to office machine dealers or
individuals. Scour the weekly "shopper" papers or the
classified ads in your daily newspaper for a good deal.
You need to find the machine that suits your style,
your skills, and has the most features for your money.

When I started my business, I narrowed my choice
to the Remington or the IBM. I was looking for a company that could accommodate my financial status as well
as my need to have the typewriter immediately. (I was
foolish enough to have placed ads before I acquired a
typewriter. I already had a customer and no machine.)
I was hoping to arrange a rent-to-purchase contract so
that I didn't waste my money on rental with no possibility of having it apply to the purchase.

The Remington and IBM correcting typewriters were
nearly identical. They were made from the same patent,
as a matter of fact. The parts were interchangeable.
The Remington did have some added features which made
it attractive to me, however, The repeating "period"
key is ideal for my academic work (tables of contents,
charts, etc.). I also appreciate the repeating "x." I
do a lot of rough drafts, and it comes in handy. That
feature is also handy when adding a simple graphics
touch to a page. Lastly, I was impressed with the variable touch control selection and the fact that the key
to activate the correcting mechanism had been moved
just a little to the right and out of the way of the
shift lever. My pinky finger is sometimes a little
wayward.

With all other things considered equal, though, I
decided for the Remington because of the favorable
rental/purchase arrangement, and because the typewriter
was available the day I gave them my down-payment. IBM
had a three-month order backlog and would not loan me a
machine for the interim (unless I wanted to pay their
rates which were higher than any other office-machine
rental business). Presented with those roadblocks,
buying the IBM was out of the question for me.

My Remington SR-101 has served me well for over 8
years now with only minor break-in adjustments that can
be expected on any new piece of machinery whether it's
a car, a typewriter, or a multi-million-dollar computer. But now that the company is out of the typewriter-
manufacturing business, I'm stuck hoping I can find
repair technicians and spare parts if I do have a problem. So far no difficulty, but one of these days I'll
be stumped.

When I bought my machine, I gave thought to the
possibility that Remington would discontinue manufacturing typewriters (as they had several years earlier with
their manual model), but even the giants fall. Some of
the little companies grow to be giants, and some of the

giants grow too fast and have a weak link somewhere that causes their downfall.

On the other hand, one of my colleagues bought an IBM. She had used one in her previous job for over 10 years. Her IBM had always given her good service, she was used to it, and she bought an IBM for her home business. She knew the name, trusted the company's reputation, and was not swayed by any of the competition. Even so, she's not without problems. For a long time IBM stopped manufacturing the Selectric II in favor of its newer Selectric III. She wasn't in exactly the same dilemma I was because there was no shortage of repair specialists or parts, and IBM has since resumed manufacture of the Selectric II. Do you suppose they listened to the thousands of secretaries who argued that the II was better than the III?

An equipment purchasing decision is a matter of personal preference. You must pick the machine that suits your needs. You may have a favorite of your own. The choice of a typewriter has to be an individual one. Look carefully at all the brands: their features; their purchase plans; their service record; their resale value; and the availability of parts, service, and supplies.

Ask for a demonstration and type on each one for 15-30 minutes. If leaving your home for a demonstration would be difficult or inconvenient, ask for a home demonstration. Any salesperson who is serious about selling a typewriter will make the effort to bring the machine to you.

A thousand dollars is a lot of money, so don't be intimidated into making a hurried decision. You are the professional, remember? Salespersons don't have the right to push you around any more than customers do. Before you commit that much money to a piece of equipment that is <u>absolutely</u> <u>vital</u> to the success of your business, look closely, ask lots of questions, and ask for written quotations on price and delivery date. Don't rely on verbal commitments from eager salespeople.

A word of caution about buying a used typewriter. According to the National Office Machine Dealers Association (NOMDA) the "selectric-style" typewriters are the hottest item on the black market -- hotter than handguns. Thousands of typewriters are stolen each year. Many of them are resold at a "bargain" to unsuspecting

individuals (or are they really) who can't pass up a
good bargain. Some thefts can't be traced because the
original owner never recorded the serial number of the
machine before it was stolen, or has misplaced the purchase agreement on which the serial number is noted.

Others, though, are traceable through the serial
number. Suppose you send your "new" "bargain" machine
for repair. Suppose the serial number checks against
the national list of stolen machines? Suppose you
never see that machine again except in court or on a
detective's desk at the police station? You'll be
embarrassed, you'll be out of work, and you certainly
don't need your name in the paper as "arrested for
receiving stolen property." If you're buying used
equipment from a private party, ask to see the original
bill of sale. It's always possible that if a business
is going bankrupt or has dissolved, you will receive a
legitimate bargain. Make sure, for your sake.

ELECTRONIC TYPEWRITER

What about an electronic typewriter -- one with a
memory? The choice today between electric and
electronic is a real tough one. More and more, the
electronic typewriter is becoming the accepted norm
simply because many manufacturers, designers, and
repair technicians feel that electronic machines are
less likely to break down than are their mechanical
electric counterparts.

Secondly, and perhaps more important, is the rapid
price drop of electronic typewriters. As their price
more closely matches the price of the standard electric
typewriter, the trend may switch to electronic more
rapidly. And when you buy an electronic machine, you
may as well spend a few hundred more dollars for one
that is enhanced with some internal memory and some
external storage capability.

How will you decide? That again depends on that
market analysis you did after reading Chapter 3. What
feels more comfortable to you? What do your customers
expect? For instance, if I were in your shoes and a
lot of my work was likely to be repetitious, I think
I'd be inclined to get an electronic typewriter. For
instance, if I did a lot of legal work where only the
names of the customers change (wills, partnership agreements, etc.), an electronic typewriter with sufficient
memory would be a wonderful timesaver.

How will you decide? That again depends on that market analysis you did after reading Chapter 3. What do your customers expect? For instance, if I were in your shoes and a lot of my work was likely to be repetitious, I think I'd be inclined to get an electronic typewriter to eliminate the possibility of error in retyping. For instance, if I did a lot of legal work where only the names of the customers change (wills, partnership agreements, etc.), an electronic typewriter with sufficient memory would be a wonderful timesaver.

However, if you were in the academic business where so much of the work is one-time in and out of the machine, electronics and memory probably wouldn't be worth the extra investment. Yes, there are times when you'll have to type a page over to correct a large error, but on the whole, it may be foolish to invest $2,000 or more right now if you don't need to or can't afford to. You can always upgrade later on. Then the typewriter will be a valuable back-up.

If you think your business can support the added expense of an electronic typewriter, and if you are familiar with its use and applications, then by all means buy it. I'm not about to discourage you. As I've said a dozen or more times, **you** do the deciding. What kind of business do you plan, how much work do you plan to do, how much money do you have to spend?

WORD PROCESSOR?

I feel that a word processor is unnecessary and impractical in the beginning of any home-based typing business -- especially one that must start on a limited budget. Most word processors cost several thousand dollars. I would be extremely reluctant to spend that much money -- or to advise you to spend that much money -- until I had a firmly established business with a long list of regular customers who would use the word-processing services enough to pay for the machine. If your budget is tight, I recommend that you start as small as you can, and then improve as your customers and workload permit.

If you have a more generous budget, and a secure customer base, and strong word processing skills, and the ability to market those skills to customers, then your equipment should be a word processor, not a typewriter. The business advice is the same, however, whether you're using a mechanical or electronic typewriter, a word processor, or a computer with word processing capability.

The three best books (of the ones I've seen so far) to read if you are considering purchasing a word processor or computer with word processing capability are:

WORD PROCESSORS AND INFORMATION PROCESSING, by Dan Poynter. Published by Para Publishing.

THE WORD PROCESSING BOOK   and
THE PERSONAL COMPUTER BOOK, by Peter McWilliams. Published by Prelude/Ballantine.

The bookshelves are swelling with new titles about computers and word processors every day. (I have one myself on how to run a word processing business at home, in addition to this one on how to run a typing business at home.) Most stores stack these books alphabetically by the author's last name, so look through the section carefully and choose the book that seems to be written in your style. I'm sure that if I revised this book every six months, I could add at least a dozen new titles each time.

*   *   *   *

The right tools can enhance your ability to do your job. But selecting the right tools is like selecting the right clothes to wear. Any piece from the inside out that doesn't match or doesn't work or doesn't fit right can throw the whole look off kilter, detract from your professionalism, cause frustration, and in this case cost you business. This is no small amount of money to be spending, so use a 4-P process. Ponder, Probe, and Plan before Purchasing or leasing.

...AND ACCESSORIES

What are the chances that your family will object strongly to the typewriter's noise? If their decibel tolerance is low, invest a few more dollars and buy a noise-reduction hood for your machine. It will cost from $10 to $50 depending upon the manufacturer and the amount of noise reduction you need.

You should definitely get a foam rubber pad for under the machine. This not only helps with the noise reduction, it also provides shock absorption for the machine and the surface it sits on, thereby cutting down on vibration.

When you purchase the machine (or when you sign a rental agreement) also ask about the "bolt-down" burglary prevention safety feature. This bolt-down process involves drilling two holes through the bottom of the typewriter case and through the desk or table on which it will be placed. Next two bolts are fastened in place with appropriate nuts and washers. Then the machine's mechanical parts are placed in the case, the cover is replaced, and <u>voila</u>, no one can move the typewriter without taking it all apart. This simple procedure will probably cost you under $10, much cheaper and perhaps more reliable than one of the fancy typewriter-security devices that are for sale.

You should have at least two different typing elements (the "ball" with the letters on it). Over the years I've accumulated seven for the different kinds of work I do. This gives me a great deal of versatility. One way it really has helped has been when I prepared papers for more than one person in any particular college class. By using three different elements, the papers looked unique and not like they'd been turned out by some pay-by-the-page underground (and illegal and unethical and unfair) report-writing service.

The standard type faces are:

1.   The Courier style that this book is typed with. This makes a clear impression and is very easy on the eyes.

2.   This Gothic style looks quite a bit like printing. Many businesses prefer this style, and it is also a favorite with people or companies that prepare technical instruction booklets or lists of rules and regulations.

3.   *Italics is used for emphasis or for a more personal touch. This is an example of Italics at 12-pitch.*

    Italics also retains its good looks when it is spread to 10-pitch. Spread out like this it is often used on invitations.

Some other common styles for special projects or different purposes are:

4.   This smaller Courier style is complimentary to the
      larger one that this book is typed with. I find
      this one useful when I am preparing tables or
      charts and don't want the typestyles to be notice-
      ably different from the text of the paper. The
      smaller character allows me to put more in less.

5.   This very spartan Artisan style is also suitable
      for putting a lot of words in a small space and
      without having the work look crowded. It is also
      useful, like the Gothic, when you wish to have a
      document look as if it were commercially printed.
      Spread to 10-pitch it begins to thin out.

6.   This Elite version of the older typestyles is
      popular with some people. It is sometimes used
      to type personal material.
      Spread to 10-pitch it is a little thin, also.

7.   This Pica element is also a great deal like
      the typestyle found on older manual type-
      writers. This element is often used on
      legal documents.

8.   THIS "ORATOR" ELEMENT HAS MANY PRACTICAL
      APPLICATIONS. IN ITS LOWER-CASE POSITION,
      IT IS EFFECTIVE FOR HEADLINES OR EMPHASIS.
      IN ITS UPPER-CASE POSITION, IT IS EXCELLENT
      FOR PREPARING SPEECHES, BUT YOU MUST LEAVE
      SPACE. THE LETTERS SOMETIMES MISS, ALSO.

     There are many more as well: for technical,
scientific, foreign language, and computer applications.

     If you rent a typewriter, the contract probably
includes one element. For practical purposes, you
should rent another one so that you have dual pica and
elite capability. My advice is to get the large
Courier style (pica or 10-pitch) and the Gothic style
(elite or 12-pitch).

     If you buy a typewriter, two elements are included
in most purchase agreements. In this case, order the
Courier and the Gothic styles with the machine, and
then buy one each of an Italics and a small Courier-12
style. Buy additional elements as you need them for
special projects or to fill a regular customer's
request.

The elements cost between $15 and $20 depending on the manufacturer and on whether you get a new one or a reconditioned one. I have had success with both.

MAINTENANCE CONTRACT

Lastly under consideration when buying a typewriter is service. When you rent one, the service will be the company's responsibility. But as soon as you buy a machine, sign up for a service contract as well. The usual warranty on a new typewriter is 90 days. At the end of that time, you need to be sure you are protected against any machine failure. An average service call from a reputable typewriter-repair shop runs $35 minimum. If you've purchased a maintenance contract -- even if it costs you $100 a year. It takes only one or two service calls (with parts, travel time, labor, etc.) and that contract has paid for itself.

At a weekly cost of a little over $2, you'd be foolish to be without protection of your most essential piece of equipment (next to your body, of course). Granted, you may not use it for 2 or 3 years. But consider it a "business interruption" insurance policy. You won't be out of business simply because you don't have the money to pay for repairs on an as-needed basis.

The average cost throughout the country for a service/maintenance contract is $80 a year. IBM charges about $90 right now. My Remington contract used to be $68. Often an independent service technician can offer equal or better service (faster, at least) at lower rates. But, before you sign up with an independent, ask for references from satisfied customers. Call them up and ask if the service was reliable and thorough and on-time. Also check into their loaner policy if your machine cannot be fixed at your desk and must be taken to the shop. And don't allow any repair technician to remove your machine from your home unless you are handed a signed receipt with the company's name professionally printed on it.

DESK & CHAIR

Initially you can "make do" by putting the typewriter on the kitchen table and sitting in whatever chair is the most comfortable. But, believe me, this will get old after only a few hours. You'll be sore,

you'll be uncomfortable, and you'll get tired more
easily. The work you turn out will begin to show all
of that fatigue before long. You'll get careless and
make errors.

You'll also get irritated very quickly when you
have to move the typewriter to eat, and move the dishes
to type. You can get around this switchy-changy for a
short while by eating on TV trays, but why go through
the extra bother? In addition, as soon as you give
your typewriter a place of its own, you will treat the
business as a real one and give it more respect.

My first major purchase (even before I had paid
for the typewriter) was a comfortable, rugged chair in
good condition. I paid $35 for it at an outlet which
sold used office furniture. My used chair held up well
for over 2-1/2 years. When the old one broke a leg, I
bought a brand new chair, and we gave the old one a
sentimental "retirement" party complete with borrowed
gold watch. The new chair has a fabric seat AND back-
rest, a big improvement and something you might seriously consider. In the summer heat, vinyl can be miser-
ably uncomfortable.

I recommend that you get a comfortable, sturdy
chair that will fit your body and your way of sitting.
You'll be spending many hours in it, so be sure it
offers comfort, support, and stability. You can eliminate a lot of back, neck, shoulder, and arm problems by
having a chair that suits you.

I was lucky that my used chair held up so well for
so long and was so comfortable. If you can find a good
used one, buy it. If not, spend the extra money for a
high-quality new chair. I borrowed a typing stand from
a friend for a few weeks until my husband constructed a
wooden platform for the typewriter that was just the
right height and had room enough for the machine and a
copy holder.

I continued with that make-shift set-up for almost
a year. When we moved to a larger house, I had room
for a full-size desk. I found a wonderful wooden
secretary's desk (one of the old oak ones with the
spring-loaded typing stand) for only $50. This gem was
advertised in the neighborhood throw-away newspaper.
Unless the desk will be right in the middle of your
living room, it doesn't need to win a decorator's
award. My used desk is actually quite ugly because of
early abuse and several poor attempts at refinishing

by its former owners. But it is covered with work so
much of the time (not to mention reference books, a
file stand, and the IN/OUT boxes), that no one really
sees it anyway. About once every six months I clean
off the top to dust, and then I can't find anything for
a week. I'm sure you know what I mean.

A few months ago I moved the whole office set-up
from the dining room corner to a now-vacant bedroom.
Because I could spare only one day to make the move
before plunging right back into the paperwork, I carefully removed all the "stuff" on the top of the desk,
placed it on the kitchen table exactly as it had been
on the desk (pile for pile). After the desk was re-
situated in the new site, I carefully transferred the
paperwork from the table to the desk. It was so slick
you'd have thought I had just beamed it into the other
room a-la Star Trek.

My advice is to get a desk and a chair at the
beginning if you can afford it and if you have enough
room. Somehow, after I bought the desk my business
took on more credibility, it was real. The business
now had its own status; it wasn't just something that
kept getting in the way or making noise during evening
television hours.

When you start looking
for a desk, check all the
thrift stores, all the
stores that sell used office
equipment, garage sales, and
tell all your friends so they
can check the ads in their
area.

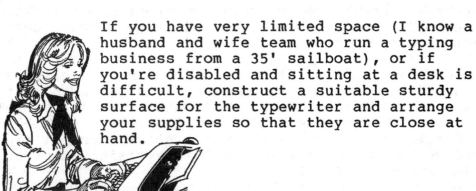

If you have very limited space (I know a
husband and wife team who run a typing
business from a 35' sailboat), or if
you're disabled and sitting at a desk is
difficult, construct a suitable sturdy
surface for the typewriter and arrange
your supplies so that they are close at
hand.

TELEPHONE

You will also need a telephone to conduct your business. It doesn't matter a whole lot in the beginning whether you use the home phone or get a separate business phone. What does matter, however, is that you have a telephone within arm's reach. I can't think of anything more aggravating than to be in the middle of a RUSH job and have to get up to answer the telephone 10 feet away -- especially if the call isn't for you.

You can solve the telephone situation in many ways: add a long cord to a telephone that you already have; have the phone company install an extension to your present instrument; or install a separate line for your business. The choice is up to you and is based on your situation and your business expectation.

For example, a single woman with teenage children would probably want a separate line for the business. A widowed woman who lives alone can manage well, though, with no additional extension at all if she can rearrange her furniture to be close to the existing telephones in her home.

Until just recently, we used our personal phone line for a business line. Initially this arrangement was fine because our younger daughter already had her own phone which she pays for herself. I decided not to get a business listing or advertise in the Yellow Pages. I preferred to operate my business on a more one-to-one basis, take referrals only, and see customers by appointment only.

I figured that if I advertised in the Yellow Pages I would be creating the possibility of walk-in customers. In addition, in order to advertise in the Yellow Pages, I HAD to have a business line which is billed at a different rate. I stuck with the residential line and depended on non-commercial advertising in other places.

With the Bell System in the midst of deregulating, all the local utilities are changing their rules as fast as they can be approved by the state utility governing agencies. Provided this approach will still work for you when you are reading this, here is one sensible way to acquire a business line and listing without being required to post a hefty deposit as a new business. There's a reason for this deposit, and it's as much to protect you as it is to protect the utility's interests. But, if you already have a residential line, why not capitalize on the good credit that line has already built up for you? Here's how:

1. First, order in a second residential line. Say it's for a teenager, for a "his 'n her" convenience, for your parents, or whatever.

2. Second, convert one of the residential lines to business service. You can convert without a deposit, but to initiate service for a new business requires a deposit. Why? Because many new businesses rack up large long-distance toll charges, have difficulty paying the bill, fold in a few months, and the phone company must write off the debt, thereby making it necessary to raise rates of existing customers who pay faithfully.

3. Next, decide which line will be business and which will be residential. Keep in mind that in most areas, you may have a dual listing (business and residential) on the business number, but you may only list personal names on a residential service.

Do you understand all of that? If not, talk casually with a service representative at your phone company. Whether it's the Bell System, General Telephone, or an independent utility, you're bound to find one helpful service representative who can advise you how to do this. If you strike out the first time, go back again (or phone again).

Keep in mind that you MUST have a business service to advertise in the Yellow Pages (you are usually entitled to a "free" one-line listing, and that may be enough for a start). Secondly, you AREN'T SUPPOSED to conduct business -- incoming and outgoing calls and widespread advertising -- using the number for a residential listing.

One caution: Don't give away your name or your present phone number in any of these preliminary discussions. Pretend to be ignorant of what I told you and just ask questions. Once they pull your record and you've told them you're in business, they may give you the business. There's no sense asking for trouble until you've figured out your strategy.

The last thing you want is an uninvited "survey" or "just checking" if you've just begun your business and are using your residential line without having converted it to business service. This isn't a jail-time offense, but utilities have a way of making little folks feel mighty intimidated, and who needs that when you're trying to build up a business?

ANSWERING DEVICE

In addition to the telephone close at hand, I recommend an answering device. As you will see when you read Chapter 9, I used mine for ensuring my privacy as well as for taking messages. In the early stages of my business, my answering machine was invaluable for being my "ears" while I was out distributing flyers and handing out business cards.

There are other ways in which an answering device will save you time and worry. My family used it to keep each other posted on individual schedules. With a husband who had on-call responsibilities and three teen-agers, for example, just planning meals was hazardous to my mental health. With the answering device, they could leave me a message even when I wasn't home.

A side benefit of my device has been a sharp decline in unpleasant phone calls. It's a sad reality in our world that once you advertise your phone number publicly, you are vulnerable to this kind of rude, cruel, and senseless intrusion. I have found, however, that deviates are reluctant to be recorded and they usually hang up.

In the beginning I purchased a very simple machine on sale at Radio Shack for right around $50. I'm certain the device has saved or made me that much money ten times over. One woman wrote to me and said that she bought a more elaborate model for over $300 that allows her to call in from her "real job" and get her messages. I thought that sounded like a good idea, particularly if you are trying to start your business while still working full-time somewhere else.

Somewhere in that vast price range is the model that will fit your needs perfectly. As with the typewriter, ask for demonstrations, see if there is a trial period available, and shop around for the best price on the model that meets your specifications. You may be able to find a good used model by watching the ads in the newspaper for new ones or by scanning the classified ads and the "shopper" papers.

TRANSCRIBER

In a medical or legal typing business, and for many business/commercial typing services, a transcriber is essential. Again, I recommend a new machine unless you can find a reconditioned one that comes with a solid guarantee.

Some of the models currently available include: Sony, Dictaphone, Sanyo, Norelco, etc. One feature that is particularly helpful on a transcriber is the automatic reverse for 1 or 2 seconds. This allows you to replay one or two words and catch your place in the dictation.

Many models are versatile and can accommodate standard cassettes as well as mini cassettes. This adaptability may be a big plus for your business if you will be doing dictation transcription for a variety of customers. You will be able to do work for the person who tapes a lecture on a standard tape recorder, and you will be able to type for the executive who dictates letters and reports in a small hand-held recorder.

Sometimes you may have to purchase what is being used by the majority of your customers, rather than what is your personal preference. For instance, many court reporters are still using Stenorette machines. If this is your specialty, you'd be foolish to buy a cassette transcriber.

In my academic typing business I received very few requests for transcription. I never enjoyed it when I had my "real job" so I just didn't plan to offer it in my business. Other women prefer transcription to typing from traditional copy. In those cases, a made-to-order home-based transcription service is absolutely ideal.

I don't think that a beginning home typing business needs to include a transcriber UNLESS that business will be almost entirely transcription. Then the machine is a necessity rather than a frill.

If you choose to include transcription services in your business, pick out a transcriber with the same care and good business sense that you used when picking out the typewriter. The transcriber is a delicate and very technical piece of machinery, and should be selected for versatility, dependability, and ease of operation. Once you have narrowed your choice of models, then dicker for the best price, maintenance contract, delivery date, etc.

A transcriber presently costs around $300. This is one item that can frequently be found in good used condition, especially by looking through the classified ads in the newspaper or by buying through reputable office-machine dealers. You might even find one at a pawn shop. If you buy from a private party, ask to have the machine checked over by an office-machine specialist before you buy. If a seller is "on the level" this is a reasonable request and you should have no trouble making that arrangement.

But do be careful. Just as with the typewriter, the black market for this equipment is very active. If the price is extraordinarily low, ask to see the original bill of sale so you won't end up losing your machine to a competent police detective.

REFERENCE BOOKS

A few well-chosen reference books on your desk will save you a lot of hours of frustration. No matter what kind of business you operate, I recommend the following:

        Webster's Collegiate Dictionary
        Roget's Thesaurus
        English Handbook (any one will do fine)
        Webster's Secretarial Handbook
        Reference Manual for Stenographers & Typists
            by Gavin Sabin (Gregg/McGraw-Hill)
        The Little English Handbook: Choices and
            Conventions, by Edward Corbett (Wiley)

*   *   *   *

For an academic typing business, style manuals and handbooks are vital. The standard ones are:

        MLA Handbook for Writers of Research Papers,
            Theses, and Dissertations

Turabian's A Manual for Writers of Term Papers,
    Theses, and Dissertations

Campbell & Ballou: Form and Style: Theses,
    Reports, Term Papers

APA Publication Manual

American Anthropologist

Council of Biology Editors Manual

A few extras for specialized applications include:

Journal of Biological Chemistry

Biochemistry

Handbook for Authors: Journal of the American
    Chemical Society

Bulletins of the Geological Society of America

Style Manual for Guidance in the Preparation
    of Papers for Journals Published by the
    American Institute of Physics

Journal of the American Sociology Association

In addition, students may bring you specific directions from an instructor. Or a university's graduate
division which is responsible for accepting all theses
and dissertations may print up a set of instructions
that are unique to that institution.

Some of the rules that differ from institution to
institution, for example, are the ways in which you
divide words. In the paragraph just above, the word
"direction" is correctly divided by all the rule books
I have on my desk, but if I had had to divide it "direction" that would have been unacceptable at two of
the five universities/colleges in my area. The way I
divided it two lines above is acceptable in the dictionary even though leaving only two letters on a line
is not recommended.

Become familiar with all the little subtle rules
and regulations by THOROUGHLY reading each school's
guidelines for graduate students and typists. This
preparation can save you many hours of re-typing (which
is at _your_ expense, since it is _your_ responsibility to

know the rules). Most of the guidelines that are
issued to students make it very clear that the student
is responsible for adhering to all format rules, but we
all know that students don't do that. They believe the
typist is responsible, so we're all better off if we
accept the responsibility graciously and raise our
prices a little to reflect that added knowledge and
responsibility.

*   *   *   *

If you plan on a business/commercial typing service, you should have all of the books I mentioned
earlier. In my reading and searching, I have found a
few more which are extremely valuable, especially if
you will be responsible for any editing of customers'
work.

The Business Writer's Handbook, by Brusaw,
        Alred, & Oliu. Published by St. Martin's
        Press, Inc.

The Dennison Zip Code Directory (available
        in stationery stores)

Write Right! and Better Letters, by Jan
        Venolia. Published by Ten Speed Press

The Complete Resume Guide, by Marian Faux.
        Published by Monarch Press.

Don't Use a Resume, Use a Qualifications Brief,
        by Richard Lathrop. Published by Ten
        Speed Press.

Resumes: The Nitty Gritty, by Joyce Kennedy.
        Published by Sun Features, Inc.

Write Better, Speak Better
        and
The Family Word Finder. Published by Reader's
        Digest, Pleasantville, New York 10570

If your business will be medical typing/transcription,
you need a comprehensive medical dictionary as well as
a medical terminology textbook or handbook.

Taber's Cyclopedic Medical Dictionary

The Medical Word Book, by Sheila Sloane.
        Published by W. B. Saunders.

The Surgical Word Book, by Claudia Tessier.
     Published by W. B. Saunders.

Dorland's Illustrated Medical Dictionary.
     Published by W. B. Saunders.

Physician's Desk Reference (PDR)

                *   *   *   *

     For legal typing and transcription, many of the
books from the two previous sections are necessary.
The following will also be very helpful for beginners
or veterans:

     Black's Law Dictionary

     A legal secretary's handbook

     Legal Secretaryship, by Norma Blackburn.
          Published by Prentice-Hall.

                *   *   *   *

     If your business is typing for either amateur or
professional writers, I recommend many of the books in
the Business Section and:

     Writer's Market, published by Writer's Digest

     The Writer's Handbook, published by The Writer

     The Craft of Fiction   and
     The Craft of Non-Fiction by Knott, published
          by Reston Publishing

     The Elements of Style, by Strunk & White,
          published by MacMillan

     The Complete Writing Guide, by Carolyn
          Mullins. Published by Prentice-Hall.

     Dear Publisher, written and published by Carol
          Shrum, P.O. Box 726, Clayton, CA

     Literary Market Place, published by R.R. Bowker.

     Complete Guide to Editorial Freelancing, by
          C. O'Neill and A. Ruder

     How to Get Happily Published, by Judith Applebaum

                    *   *   *   *

    If you run into any special problem that none of
these books can solve, you still have some options.
Ask the customer if he or she has any additional reference material that can help you with layout, terminology, format, etc.

    In addition, take advantage of the wealth of infor-
mation available in your public library. I know that
I've been giving the library a lot of "plugs" in this
book, but you have no idea how many times the men and
women at the reference desk have helped me out of a
predicament. They have spent hours researching things
with me -- for this book and for customers' work. They
are highly trained and have saved me hours of time primarily because they know where to look whereas I could
spend a whole afternoon just figuring out which book to
look in for the information that I need.

SUPPLIES

    The next best friend that your business can have
is the local stationery store owner or clerk. On a
rush job, having the right tools and supplies close at
hand will make the difference between frustration and
elation.

    Always keep your supplies replenished. Because I
often typed in the evening or on weekends, I made sure
I had staples, paper, typewriter ribbons and correcting
tapes, and envelopes. Post a shopping list right next
to your typewriter so you never run out of anything or

                            86

forget what it was you were supposed to pick up at the stationery store.

When selecting a stationery store for your regular purchases, contact all of them and compare prices on a few standard items. Ask if any of the stores offer a further discount to businesses such as yours. The store with initially higher prices might turn out to be less expensive in the long run if it offers a discount to regular customers. Also, a stationery store that offers delivery service is invaluable to you. That service may be worth an extra nickel or two on some items, particularly when you're on deadline.

Build up a good working rapport with the owner or the senior clerk. This will work two ways. First, you will be pleased with their service and the quality of their merchandise, so will likely refer some of your customers to them. Second, they will become familiar with your business and your warm enthusiasm and will send you customers. They will also be very willing to put a little extra effort into obtaining an out-of-stock item when you need it desperately.

The supplies that you will need for a very basic start are:

> pen, pencil, package of inexpensive paper
> (xerographic), correction fluid, and ruler,
> extra ribbon and correction tape

In a couple of weeks, or after your first $30 of profit (after expenses), start a list of the things you reached for but didn't have:

> stapler (including staples and staple remover),
> scissors, 3-hole punch, letter opener, large
> eraser, scotch tape, paper clips, receipts

With the next few dollars of profit, go back for:

> a copy stand, magnifying glass, more typewriter
> ribbons and correcting tapes, 3 x 5 cards or an
> address book, rubber cement, thumb tacks, scratch
> pads, large plain envelopes, dictionary, pencil
> sharpener, stationery tray for the desk drawer

After you get really moving along and have built up quite a nest egg in your 10% Re-investment Budget, start thinking about a carpet protector for under your chair, a good light for your work area, and a small

calculator for figuring customer's bills and your grow-
ing bank balance.

An item I added just recently was a desk-top vertical file to separate incoming work from finished work.
I use the other spaces for my personal work and one for
miscellaneous sheets of reference material.

Would you buy office supplies from a mail order
catalog? I would if the price were right and at least
a dozen other people recommended the firm to me. There
are at least six or seven reputable mail-order office
supply firms in this country, possibly more, but I
haven't heard of all of them yet. You'll hear from
them as soon as your new business name shows up on a
few mailing lists, so I won't go to the trouble of
listing them here. Addresses may change, and what's
worse than writing a letter and getting it back in the
mail?

Shopping can be fun when you've earned the money
yourself.

CHAPTER 6
Legal Details

So, now that you've decided this venture is for you, you've identified a market for your skills, and you've solved all your money and equipment problems, you're all ready. Well, almost. There are a few legal details to deal with. None are major hurdles, and not all of them are necessary depending on your business and your local rules, but all of the issues are worthy of note and consideration for any new business.

BUSINESS NAME

Will you be Mary Jones or "Jones Professional Typing"? Will you be "Sincerely Yours" or would you prefer "Speed-o-gram Secretarial" or Sandy Smith? The decision to use your given name or a fictitious name is sometimes emotional and sometimes practical (and sometimes for tax avoidance purposes by using your own name and dealing only in cash). Let's explore the issues.

What kind of business will you be operating and how widely will you advertise it? If you choose an academic service catering to a small clientele for 15 hours a week, you may be more comfortable using your own name. Doctors and dentists use their own names for their professional service businesses. For example, let's pretend that someone named Mary McDonald, D.D.S. sees patients one at a time in her own office and is not part of a large medical/dental group practice. She did, however, incorporate for liability and certain tax reasons.

Suppose you will also be seeing clients one at a time, by appointment, and you will offer individual service as opposed to a large-scale operation. You may choose to conduct your business using your given name with the qualifying, "Professional Typist."

If you choose a business or commercial typing and secretarial service that caters to small or medium firms, you will be wise to adopt a fictitious business name. Businesses prefer to deal with businesses, even though the individuals in those businesses are the most important components. How do you choose a name? Are you creative or location oriented? Are you the "Word Expert" or are you "Broadway Typing Service" whose interest feature is, "I'm a word expert!" Is your location important? "Lakeside Office Services" is probably on the lake or in a neighborhood that is referred to as Lakeside. To a merchant in the area, a landmark may be important. Are you "Tower Secretarial" referring to a local clock or school tower in town?

I can't tell you how to name your business. The process is up to you, as are most of the decisions about running your business. Perhaps these examples have set your brain in gear?

Consider these four simple guidelines when selecting a business name. Choose carefully because you'll live with it a long time. Changing your business name involves repeating the following processes all over. I know. I named my publishing company hastily, and conducted business under an embarrassing and difficult-to-pronounce name for 2 years before being able to change it. Some people haven't let me live it down yet.

1. Is the name easy to say, understand, and remember?

2. Does the name accurately reflect what you do?

3. Does the name limit what you do, or give you room to grow and expand?

4. Does the name fit you?

*   *   *   *

If you've chosen a fictitious business name (and second and third choices if your first is already taken), now you must record that name in the public documents. The procedure for this differs from state to state, from city to county to parish and township. Start with your town offices, your city hall, or your county clerk. Most business name filings are done on a state level, and business licenses are handled on a local level. If the registration procedure is state-wide, a local agency probably handles the paperwork for the state.

Registering your business name is usually done for one of two reasons (or both). One, to protect the customer. A fictitious business name is just that: fictitious. A consumer must have some way of tracing the owner and responsible person in case of any dispute. Second, to protect the business owner. If your name is registered, no one else may use exactly the same name, and no one but you or someone you designate may conduct business under that name or sign checks made out to that name.

After you've filed your fictitious business name, you must usually publish it. This custom dates back to English common law, before America was settled. Publishing your business name establishes your identity in the eyes and mind of the consumer, makes you legitimate, allows all the world to see who owns "Main Street Secretarial," and proclaims that you are now "OPEN FOR BUSINESS." "Publishing" your fictitious name involves placing a legal notice in a newspaper which receives general circulation in the area in which you will be doing business. The agency which accepts your fictitious name statement will also be able to provide you with a list of acceptable newspapers in which to publish that statement. You are also now on hundreds of mailing lists and will receive at least a wastebasket full of junk mail. Read it all, though, some of it may be helpful or may provide a lead on a new client.

FORM OF BUSINESS

The simplest, oldest, least regulated, and most common form of business is a sole proprietorship. As the term implies, only one person (or in some states a husband and wife) owns and is operating a business. One person makes all the decisions and can terminate the business whenever she or he chooses. This form of business arrangement will suit perhaps 97% of the home-based typing businesses. Tax reports from a sole proprietorship are filed right along with personal income taxes at the end of the year as discussed earlier in the section on Taxes. A tax consultant can assist you in filling in the Schedule C of the 1040 tax return. As sole proprietor, you are completely responsible for all debts and obligations which are incurred in the business name.

Another option, particularly if two people plan to go into business together, is a partnership. Do be careful, though. Friends are great, but they are often poor business partners. Solid long-standing friend-ships have disintegrated in the middle of arguments over business decisions or money. The tax and banking situations are a little different, and the funds are controlled a bit more stringently. The debts of one partner are automatically the debts of the other.

When considering a partnership, consult an attor-ney and enter into a formal signed agreement. In that document, clearly spell out each partner's responsi-bility, authority, liability limit, capital investment, and profit or loss share. Also include the arbitration or litigation method for settling disagreements, the procedures for a partner to withdraw or be added, and how the accumulated assets will be split when and if the partnership ceases operation.

Incorporation is impractical for all but a very few typing or secretarial services. The main reason for incorporating is to protect your personal assets from attack in case of wrong doing or liability. Cor-porations operate on a fiscal year that may or may not coincide with the traditional calendar year. I frankly don't think incorporating offers enough advantages to outweigh the administrative and paperwork headaches it creates.

The major drawback to incorporation is that the business is taxed on two levels: one, the organiza-tion's profits are taxed; and two, income the individ-uals receive from the business is also taxed. Incorpor-ating your business is also very expensive and subject to endless government regulation. Before deciding on a partnership or on incorporation, consult a tax attor-ney.

BUSINESS LICENSE

Within a week of filing your fictitious business name you should also acquire a business license in your jurisdiction. These may or may not be the same. For instance, where I live, the county clerk accepts

92

fictitious name filings for the State of California, yet the City of Huntington Beach issues my business license. This simple process might be sticky and might be impossible where you live, though. I've heard of some real Catch-22 situations.

Let's discuss the easy, straight-forward way first. Present yourself and your fictitious name registration to the business license bureau in your town, city, or county. Fill out the forms, pay the annual fee, smile and say "Thank you," and go home and turn on the typewriter. Oh, that they were all so simple.

Suppose your neighborhood does not permit you to run a business from home? Or, you are allowed to operate a business at home if you don't have customers, don't allow trucks, don't advertise, and don't make noise or a mess. In my city, my particular block was zoned for "limited professional business." There's an accountant down the block and there's me.

All I needed to do to obtain my license and permission was to go to another section of city hall, sign a zoning variance stating that I would not permit undue traffic or big trucks, and take that variance back to the business license clerk. There was no extra fee for this variance, and no need for a public hearing. I don't have "customers," but occasionally "friends" drop by, eh?

In a neighboring city, a woman paid $100 for the zoning variance application, then notice of the variance application was sent to all her neighbors, then she was summoned to appear at a hearing of the zoning authority. She was frightened to death until a fellow businesswoman assured her that it was unlikely any of the neighbors would object, that the hearing was only to make the variance a matter of public record, and that the $100 was the city's way of raising extra funds.

One other couple in Arizona applied for a license for their home-based typing business. They were told that the city had no procedure for licensing businesses that operated in homes, but also told them that it was illegal to conduct a business in the city without a license. This couple was determined to operate within the law, but finally gave up. One of these days their city will see the revenue possibilities in licensing home-based businesses.

As with dealing with any of the utility companies, if you face a stone wall such as this, often the easiest way around the wall is just to hush up and back up and operate in its shadow. To protect yourself, document your activities in a journal or in a letter to your own file, so that if the authorities question you later you can say, "Well I talked to this person on this day at this location and was told this and this." You're covered -- and they're covered with egg.

BUSINESS CHECKING ACCOUNT

Armed with your receipt for filing your fictitious name, you're now ready to open your business checking account. You are not allowed to open a standard business account using that fictitious name until you present proof of having filed the necessary papers. Banking regulations differ from state to state, so the following are guidelines only.

Almost all the business experts advise that you open a separate checking account for all business transactions: for income and for expenses. In a sole proprietorship business, YOU are the primary signer on the account. From my personal experience, I advise adding a second person as authorized to sign on that account. You never know when you'll be temporarily disabled, or tied up with an appointment, or travelling on business. In any of these circumstances, a second person can conduct business for you. Obviously this second person must be someone you trust.

If you have chosen to operate your business using your own given name, business experts still advise opening a separate checking account for the business. Even though the money all goes to one source, you will be able to see at a glance (and prove at a glance) what money came into the business and what expenses were paid by the business simply by leafing quickly through the pages of the checkbook. To pay yourself, simply write a check to "CASH" or to your other checking account.

What kinds of checks will you choose? Those that will fit in your budget and will conform to your style of doing business. For a very limited business with limited monthly expenses and no charge accounts at printers or copy shops, a small checkbook is perfect and the least expensive. It'll fit right in your purse or pocket making it easy to buy supplies without lugging around a big ring-bound checkbook. For a large operation that has payroll, monthly bills, a charge account at the stationery store, and an elaborate book-keeping system, large checks -- perhaps the style with a strip of carbon behind the payee's name and dollar amount -- are more appropriate and more efficient.

Balance your checking account each month as soon as it arrives and report any discrepancies immediately. Disputes are difficult to resolve when they're 6 months old. In addition, you'd be very embarrassed if you bounced a check because of a math error.

Retain your bank statements and cancelled checks for a minimum of 3 years. After 3 years the IRS statute regarding income tax audits expires. I'm one of those extra cautious folks who keeps the records just one more year "in case." I've never had an "in case," but my scout leader trained me well a long time ago.

ACCEPTING CREDIT CARDS

Accepting payment from a customer via credit card -- MasterCard or Visa -- may eliminate a certain portion of bad checks, and may encourage use of your services by a starving student who can only afford that dissertation typing on credit. On the whole, this is a simple registration procedure. Check with the loan officer or vice president of your local bank branch.

The only drawback to accepting credit card payments is that the bank charges you a fee, somewhere between 4% and 6% to act as the intermediary between you, your bank, your customer's bank, and your customer. The procedure is excellent for dealing with long-distance writer clients. If you feel that you would substantially increase your business by accepting credit cards, do it. If you feel it would be just another bother, avoid it.

COLLECTING ON BOUNCED CHECKS

Immediately phone the customer when you receive notification from your bank that a customer's check has been returned for insufficient funds. If you are unable to reach the customer by phone, send a certified letter. All you need is proof of delivery. Don't hassle the customer at his or her place of employment, or

call at an unreasonable hour of the day. If your bank
has charged you a fee for the bad check, instruct the
customer to reimburse you for that fee.

DO NOT RETURN THE CANCELLED CHECK until the debt
is satisfied. Occasionally a customer will say, "Well,
just send me back the bad check and I'll send you a new
one." NO WAY! That bounced check in your hand is your
only evidence of the crime, and yes, knowingly passing
a bad check is a crime, usually a felony.

If the customer's next check clears, or if he or
she sends a money order or cashier's check to replace
the bad one, cheerfully tear up the bad check and throw
it away. Errors can happen; they separate the humans
from the rest of the zoo. The customer may have made a
simple addition or subtraction error. The bank may
have made an error. Be cheerful if this is the explanation you receive: and just to be safe, ask for cash the
next time.

SOCIAL SECURITY NUMBER

If you don't already have a Social Security number, this is easy to obtain and will offer the least
intrusion into your personal or business life. To file
for a Social Security number, phone your nearest IRS or
Social Security office and ask the clerk to send you
the appropriate form (#SS-5). You may also do this in
person if an office is close. Fill it out, provide
proof of your birth, and it's done.

FEDERAL IDENTIFICATION NUMBER (FIN)

Unless you plan to hire employees, you probably
won't need one of these. The federal and state taxing
agencies keep track of you very nicely by using your
Social Security number.

To obtain a FIN, complete IRS form #SS-4. Again,
you may do this in person or by a combination of the
telephone and the mail. Once you are assigned a FIN,
you will automatically receive quarterly and annual
payroll deduction tax forms which you must complete and
send back, even if you don't have employees. Why go to
the bother of filing for a FIN if you have no employees? You can't ignore the form and expect the IRS to
know that you don't have employees. They don't read
minds, only paper.

SALES TAX PERMIT/RESALE PERMIT

These two names are often used interchangeably. Unless you live in a state which does not have a sales tax, you are required by law to collect sales tax for some of the services you provide. The laws vary from state to state, so inquire carefully. Basically, services are not taxed, labor is not taxed, but expendable goods, products, or end results are taxed. Most typing services are not taxable, some word-processing functions are taxable, services such as translating or editing are not taxable, yet end results such as graphic arts are taxable. The interpretations of what is a service and what is a product also vary from state to state, so I'm not willing to do any more here than to tell you to check the rules where you live.

As stated before, pretend you are dense and ignorant when you start inquiring. Don't give your name or location until you have all the facts and rules and regulations clearly figured out. Then, if it turns out that you do need a resale permit, change roles and be an in-charge busineswoman who is "here to fill out the forms and get on with the process."

One little tip: when estimating your yearly taxable sales -- only the portion that you will collect tax on -- estimate low to avoid posting a hefty deposit and/or being required to file forms quarterly. Nearly any home-based typing business that collects sales tax will collect so little that the lump sum at the end of the year will be less than $100. Only a small percentage of your annual income (sales) will be taxable (we're talking about sales-taxable to the consumer, not income taxable).

A resale permit also allows you to purchase goods without paying sales tax on them. HOWEVER, you are only exempt from paying sales tax on those goods which you will eventually re-sell in a taxable capacity. Hence the name, "resale permit." Abuse of your resale permit will mean revocation of the permit and possible criminal charges.

INSURANCE

We've already discussed health insurance and disability insurance, now's the time to consider a few more types. These first two may be offered through

your standard homeowner's or renter's policy. Ask your
agent for details. Be sure to make it very clear to
the agent that you want insurance for your business,
not for personal items. If you already have homeowner's or tenant's insurance, be sure that any
business use or materials or equipment is covered. If
you don't have an agent, ask a friend for a recommenda-
tion. Sometimes an independent agent is in a better
position to shop around and find you the best coverage
for the money you can pay.

1. **Fire Insurance.** For just a minute, consider
   how financially devastated you'd be if fire
   struck your home. Not only would you lose
   your home and personal possessions, you'd
   also be out of business. Fire loss is not
   certain, it's a maybe. The destruction toll
   is also a maybe. It could be as low as a
   couple hundred dollars; it could be several
   thousand dollars.

   Fire insurance is a certain. For a given
   premium payment, you receive a given amount
   of loss coverage. You'd be extremely foolish
   to pass up the investment and take your
   chances. Whether you own or rent, sign up
   for fire insurance -- NOW!

2. **Burglary, robbery, theft, vandalism
   insurance.** Remember that hot equipment we
   talked about in the last chapter? What would
   happen if yours were stolen, if someone
   vandalized your home and smashed up your
   furniture? You'd be out of business again,
   just as in number 1 above. Granted this
   policy usually has a deductible amount that
   you must pay before the insurance company
   pays, but it's worth it.

   I'm going to tease you. Do you know the difference between burglary, robbery, and theft?
   Attend a Neighborhood Watch meeting in your
   community and ask.

Theoretically, operating a business from home
should be very simple and straight-forward. But just
suppose some customer came into your home and was
up-ended by a misplaced roller skate or toy truck?
Broke a hip? Broke an arm? Sued you to recover the
damages from medical bills and acute mental distress
and inconvenience? Now you see why you need:

3.   **Liability Insurance.** Again, there may be a
     provision for this in your present policy.
     Check to be sure. If there isn't, there
     should be. If you have no policy, consider
     adding this option when you discuss a com-
     plete package with an agent.

If either a fire or a thief (or burglar or robber)
forces you to close your business for a week or more,
how will you pay your bills and eat? You're not disabled (unless you were injured in the fire or robbery),
so your disability insurance won't pay the bills. So:

4.   **Business Interruption Insurance** will provide
     coverage for a very small premium. When plan-
     ning your total business insurance package,
     don't leave this out. When investigating
     business interruption insurance be sure it
     includes a provision for extra expenses such
     as immediately renting new equipment or find-
     ing a new location and that it gives you
     enough time to accomplish rebuilding your
     business. A week may not be enough, a month
     is more realistic.

Most of these insurance options are plain good
sense. Others will be mandatory depending on one or
more circumstances. If a bank is loaning you a lot of
money, they'll demand that the merchandise or equipment
be insured and they may ask that your life be insured.
An auto finance company or leasing company will demand
insurance as well as protection for their investment
until the merchandise you purchased is paid for.

5.   **Life Insurance.** One more very important item
     is insurance on you. What happens to your
     business if you die? Will your spouse, child-
     ren, or parents be able to pay off your
     debts? Beyond that, what happens to your
     spouse, children, or parents if your business
     was providing them with an income? Yes, life
     insurance. At least three times your antici-
     pated annual income (before expenses) PLUS
     any debt obligation. If you earn $15,000 and
     owe $10,000, then purchase at least $60,000
     worth of insurance. That's a pittance, but
     it's better than nothing.

That's all. You should be busy for at least a
week or so making all the arrangements.

ADVERTISEMENT

Advertisements contain the only truths to be relied on in a newspaper.

— THOMAS JEFFERSON, 1819

Blow your own horn -- even if you don't sell a clam.

It pays to advertise.

— AMERICAN PROVERBS
No date, no known author

When business is good it pays to advertise; when business is bad, you've got to advertise.

— AUTHOR UNKNOWN

If you don't advertise, no one will know you exist. You are your own best (or worst) advertisement.

— PEGGY GLENN, 1982

CHAPTER 7
Advertising for the Work

Once you have thoroughly evaluated your personal situation, your skills and the available markets, the amount of money you can spend and what prices you will charge, what equipment you will have on hand to start your business, and all the legal steps necessary to begin, the next key to your success lies in effective advertising.

How well and how thoroughly you advertise in the beginning will determine how prosperous you are. You must put a lot of effort into an aggressive advertising program at the start. Notice that I said a lot of effort, not a lot of money. Quality time and careful thought are more critical than a large bank balance. After your initial work, you will probably be able to rely on word-of-mouth referrals and repeat customers. This is always the best kind of advertising, so you want to ensure that your first actions have a snowball effect.

The keys to successful advertising are: be traditional, be creative, and be there -- all at the same time. Translated, that means: follow the accepted rules, then bend them to add something that is uniquely you, and then put your words or yourself where they will be read or seen by the people who will "have to have" what you offer.

The advertising guidelines that I will give you stress the importance of personal contact. That is the ideal way, but by no means the only way. If you are restricted in your mobility, you can accomplish an acceptable level of personal contact by using the mail and the telephone in tandem.

YOUR PERSONAL IMAGE

You are your own BEST (or worst) advertisement.
To many of you, the next paragraphs will seem like
common-sense advice that never needed to be included in
this book. However, in visiting around the country, in
speaking to large groups, in receiving mail or phone
calls from hundreds of people -- I MUST INCLUDE THIS
ADVICE. Too many people don't have enough common
sense, or haven't looked in the mirror lately, and a
gentle reminder here will keep all of us on our best
behavior and looking and sounding our business-owner
best in an environment that won't embarrass us.

A telephone call is likely to be your first contact with a client. Have you ever listened to your
voice? Is it whiny, soft or child-like, curt or
choppy, raspy? Is it smooth, authoritative, warm,
friendly? To find out, tape record yourself, play it
back, and decide if you enjoy what you hear. You may
be very surprised. Most people have no idea of how
they sound. Many don't even recognize their own voice.
Are you pleased with what you hear? If not, can you
change it on your own? Perhaps a speech therapist can
help you identify your problem. You might also enroll
in a public speaking class at the community college.
Try placing a mirror in front of you and smiling when
the phone rings. It's almost impossible to sound
grouchy on the phone when smiling at such a successful
businesswoman in the mirror.

Why does it matter? When you call a friend, you
may not be negatively or positively influenced by his
or her voice. But when you phone a business, your
first and lasting impression of that business is the
telephone contact. You remember if the person you
spoke to was vague or sure, was friendly or rude, was
whiny or self-assured. If you've called a roofer to
repair a major leak, and the person on the phone seems
completely disinterested, you call another roofer. You
have an emergency and you want someone who cares.
Transpose that circumstance to a customer who calls
with an important proposal that needs to be typed.
Will you care, will you be on time; does your voice
advertise that you care and will be on time?

When the customer arrives for the appointment, how
cheerfully do you greet him or her? Do they know you
are pleased to see them? How do you look? How does
your home look? Are things under control or chaotic?
You needn't dress for Madison Avenue, nor look like a

model, nor usher the client into a decorator's dream? The basic requirements are neat and clean.

First, greet all customers at the door with a smile and a handshake -- a firm, but warm handshake. Be on time, even if the client isn't. Be ready early in case the client's schedule changes.

Second, dress appropriately. This means no faded jeans, no shorts or halter or bathing suit, no robe and slippers, no hair rollers, no attire that would negatively reflect on your professional typing ability.

Third, usher the client into a home that appears to have a degree of organization and cleanliness since that is how the client expects the work to be done -- with organization, on time, and cleanly. Leaping dogs, nuzzling cats, and clinging children should be restrained during all contacts you have with clients. Yes, you work at home, but you are in control, remember? If a screaming toddler is likely to be a problem at 4 p.m., then don't schedule client appointments at 4 p.m.

ADVERTISING PRINCIPLES

Trying to explain the principles of effective advertising in a few paragraphs or a few pages is like trying to put someone on the moon using a slingshot. Advertising executives spend years in college learning the psychology of advertising; the effects of color, line, and design; writing effective copy; print vs. radio vs. television; direct mail vs. newspaper.

What I will try to do is skim over the main and most essential elements and refer you to more books and experts for an in-depth look if you need additional ideas or advice.

My favorite theory of advertising is the A-B-C method. All advertising you do should be designed to:

A - ATTRACT new customers

B - BROADEN and BIND your existing customer base

C - CULTIVATE new customers through present ones

When you design a business card, do you want that card to attract new customers, to inform present customers of all of your services, or to be passed around by existing customers who will hand it to another associate, or all of the above?

ATTRACT - If you presented your card to a total stranger, would it convince her/him to use your services? Does it catch their attention? reel 'em in?

BROADEN - If many of your customers are first-timers, you need a card that will inform them of all the services you offer so they'll come back to you with a wide variety of work.

BIND - If you have plenty of business, your card should be designed only to remind present customers of what you do, provide them with something for their address file, and tell them what you do in case they forget.

CULTIVATE - If many of your customers are one-time customers and would not have a need to return, you want your card to be passed to their colleagues and associates (or dorm mates) who would need you. I realize that's a very simple explanation of the application of ATTRACT, BROADEN and BIND, and CULTIVATE to business-card design, but I'm sure you can see beyond the simplicity.

*   *   *   *

Another accepted theory in advertising, particularly with regard to written or spoken copy (words) on a card, a flyer, a display ad or a spoken ad is the A-I-D-A formula.

A - ATTRACT your reader/listener

I - INTEREST him or her by appealing to a need

D - stimulate DESIRE by listing benefits

A - demand ACTION with a guarantee, an offer

How does that translate to a business card? Let's dream one up. First use some interesting graphics, or snazzy card stock, or an innovative lettering style. That's your ATTRACTION. Second does your company name or description identify that you can solve that customer's need. How about "Editing my specialty: typing my love." The customer knows you are the answer to her/his editing dilemma, and also knows you'll care

about the work from start to finish. That's your
INTEREST. You are also "dependable, confidential, and
have 15 years' experience" -- your BENEFITS to him/her.
Lastly, say, "Call NOW for appointment!" There's your
ACTION. The finished product is below.

        (Yes, without writing to me for permission, you
may use all or parts of this card. It's my own design,
and I would rather give blanket permission now than
have to answer each letter individually. However, you
do owe it to yourself to try and be creative on your
own. Your own ideas are often better than anyone
else's because only you know yourself and your market.)

        Enlarged, this
also makes an effec-
tive 3 x 5 card for
posting on bulletin
boards. In this
way, you can make
one piece of art-
work serve two
functions.

        One last tidbit of information regarding what
you'll say in your telephone campaign, letter-writing,
flyer, or business card. A recent study by researchers
at Yale University has identified the following 12 most
persuasive words. discovery, easy, guarantee, health,
love, money, new, proven, results, safety, save, and
you. Use the ones that fit your style and your
business. Could someone **save** time and or **money** by
using you, and are you **easy** to find and will you
guarantee your **proven** work.

COLOR IN ADVERTISING

        Fantasize for a minute. What color: is your favo-
rite? motivates you to act? soothes your jangled
nerves? makes you feel strong and powerful? Would you
suppose that those same emotional connections apply to
flyers or business cards? You're right, they do. Here
again, is a three-semester course in a few paragraphs.

        Bright colors command attention and/or action.
Red, orange, and bright yellow top the list of the com-
manders. Greens and blues and pale colors have a

soothing effect. Sometimes the combination of a red ink on a white paper with accompanying black or blue ink will give complementary messages.

Certain colors produce almost automatic emotional associations: red with boldness and power, blue with hope and patience (dark blue is authority), green suggests foliage or money, bright yellow denotes sun while pale yellow suggests relaxation or children, orange with either fresh fruit or exuberance. Purple or violet are viewed as either royalty or extreme femininity; pink is also unmistakably feminine. Brown is associated differently by men and women: men visualize wood, leather, some sports; women see animals or perceive stability and ruggedness. Black ink is usually non-controversial, while large black spaces with white ink (or letters reversed from a white background) may mean doom, destruction, overwhelming power.

And you thought you'd just whip up a flyer and take it to the printer and put it on any old paper? Maybe there's a reason why you'd choose one color of ink or one color of paper over another. Now, I'm sure that there are color theorists who would argue with some of the associations and inferences above. Whenever a theory is presented, counter-theories spring forth ten-fold. In truth, the above list is a composite of several schools of thought on color and its impact on human behavior and decisions. If you agree, use some of it; if you disagree, use your own best instincts. These are not my original ideas, merely ideas I've picked up in the last 15 years or so. I've always been fascinated by it and thought it would provide a little light break from all this heavy talk about being in business.

For more advice on how to effectively use color in your advertising, visit a college library or your own library and browse through some of the basic books on color, particularly the sections dealing with the psychology of color and the use of color in advertising.

GENERAL ADVERTISING -- On Paper

BUSINESS CARD

Your business card should convey the impression that you are a professional. The ones on the opposite page are samples of the many ways you can design your card to suit your needs. I'm particularly impressed with

S. O. S.
Shoemaker Office Services
25381 G. Alicia Pkwy. Ste. 304
~~████~~ Hills, CA ~~████~~

~~███~~ / 951-0766

Lucy Shoemaker

Word Processing ~ Bookkeeping ~ Calligraphy

ANDERSON TYPING SERVICE

Legal, theses, statistical, manuscript,
resume and business typing

Sharon Anderson
Professional Typist   NE
                            (402)

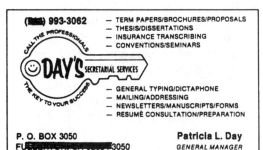

(~~███~~) 993-3062

CALL THE PROFESSIONALS
THE KEY TO YOUR SUCCESS

☺ DAY'S SECRETARIAL SERVICES

— TERM PAPERS/BROCHURES/PROPOSALS
— THESIS/DISSERTATIONS
— INSURANCE TRANSCRIBING
— CONVENTIONS/SEMINARS

— GENERAL TYPING/DICTAPHONE
— MAILING/ADDRESSING
— NEWSLETTERS/MANUSCRIPTS/FORMS
— RESUMÉ CONSULTATION/PREPARATION

P. O. BOX 3050
FU~~████████████~~3050

Patricia L. Day
GENERAL MANAGER

STENORETTE & CASSETTE
TRANSCRIBING - TYPING
DEPOSITIONS - LEGAL
STATISTICAL - MEDICAL
BUSINESS - PERSONAL

Travel Arrangements

AIRLINES
CRUISES
TOURS

BONNIE URSINI
SECRETARIAL SERVICE

8700 HUMMINGBIRD AVE.
~~████~~ VALLEY, CA ~~████~~   ~~(714)~~ 968-4844

Word Broker

~~████~~ 574-2017
Res.

JOAN SAUCERMAN
IPTN Member

Professional Typing and Secretarial Services.

D. J. HERRERA
PROFESSIONAL TYPIST

~~████~~ 963-5541
BY APPOINTMENT

BUSINESS/PUBLICATION/
MANUSCRIPT PRODUCTION

Peggy Glenn
Professional Typist

~~(714) 555-1525~~
BY APPOINTMENT

924 MAIN STREET
HUNTINGTON BEACH, CA 92648

Professional
TYPING
MaryAnn Mack

287-7012

Sharon Anderson's card. The fact that it is type-written adds to its impact. You can't tell by the copy in this book, but she has had it printed on very high-quality textured card stock. It is very effective.

Lucy Shoemaker did the calligraphy for her card. Ordinarily, this idea wouldn't work so well for a typing service, but Lucy also offers calligraphy, so it's a natural. She reports a good response. My card is actually the second one I designed. This second one advises "by appointment only," which I found to be an effective way to discourage drop-ins.

Where will you go to have business cards printed? Any one of several places, depending on your budget and the availability of services in your area. There are several huge firms which produce "boiler plate" business cards as a service for printers, stationers, and just about anyone who will take orders for these firms. The majority of cards produced this way are acceptable, reasonably inexpensive, and sufficient for an information-only approach.

One small drawback to purchasing business cards from a catalog operation such as this is that you may be placed on a junk mail list -- not by the person you order the cards from, but by the printer who produces the cards.

If you prefer to use some graphics or an original design, search for a graphic artist, design shop, or typesetting/graphics shop. Check your Yellow Pages, ask for referrals from printers or from friends. Call a few artists to compare prices, visit them to see samples of their work, and be prepared with a few ideas of your own that you'd like to see someone refine or expand. THEN, find a printer who will print your custom cards. The printing cost won't be significantly higher, you'll spend a little more for the graphics or typesetting, but you may be dollars ahead if your cards will attract more attention and bring in more business.

I hate to sound like a broken record, but this is another of those decisions that will be based on your financial resources, the creative resources in your community, and your own ideas in designing a card. I can give you ideas and direction, but you must make the decision.

I have a large collection of cards from typists throughout the country. Send yours to me when you can.

FLYER/BROCHURE

A colorful and informative flyer describing your services is another important part of your advertising strategy. A one-page, one-side flyer is the most effective in the academic or business fields, but can be equally effective in the other three fields as well.

You can post a full-size sheet in most places, but in other places where space is limited, you'll be restricted to a half sheet or smaller. I designed my flyer to be used on bulletin boards, and then I had the lower tear-out sections perforated so that customers didn't need to take the flyer down to remember my name and what I did. One woman wrote that she "perforated" her flyer by using a seamstress' pattern tracing wheel. The task was done by hand on every flyer, but she had the time and saved a chunk of money by doing it herself rather than having the printer do it.

I also have a large collection of advertising flyers and brochures from all around the country. If you're proud of yours, send it along for my file. I may not write you a long letter, but I'm always delighted at the wealth of creativity out there.

When I printed my first flyer, I chose a bright lime-green color to attract attention. As you remember, my market was the academic sector. I needed to compete in the bulletin-board world of rock-concert posters, free-clinic announcements, and homecoming queen endorsements. I feel that the typewritten flyer adds credibility to my work as a typist. I later refined the original design, incorporated a few graphic elements, and still retained the typewritten format. Both versions are shown on the next two pages. Which do you like better?

To post copies on the bulletin boards at various campuses, I first obtained permission from the college activities office. Then, armed with a staple gun and a roll of masking tape, I made the rounds of the colleges about once a semester. I soon found out, however, that I was wasting my time. Competitors removed the flyers, satisfied clients removed them (no one else can have my typist), rain destroyed them, wind blew them off, and janitors were instructed to strip the boards every 6 weeks.

I coped with these developments in a couple of ways. I enlisted a few students to re-post signs.

This flyer covers a standard 8-1/2 x 11 piece of paper, but for the purposes of this book, it has been photographically reduced to fit into the space. You can see in this instance that it's passable. It does the job. Except for the stars and headline, the flyer was done on the typewriter. To achieve the bolding effect, strike over the words several times.

☆ PROFESSIONAL ACADEMIC TYPIST ☆

15 years' experience as university secretary, now free-lance.

Hourly rate includes:
paper, cover, spelling accuracy, help with punctuation,
and editorial help as requested.

Academic manuscripts and formats my specialty.
From freshman level to post-doctoral and faculty.

Will do charts, tables, graphs, etc. No art work.

No job is too large or too small.
I've done it all from letters to reports to theses to books.
Also do scientific papers and manuscripts for professional journals.
References and examples upon request.

Research assistance, library searches, abstracting also available.

Resume development, curriculum vitae, biographical sketches.

NOTE: If you hand-write your paper, use every other line.
It's easier for me to read, so much faster and less costly to type.

PEGGY GLENN   Huntington Beach   **714/000-0000**

TYPING PRO	**TYPING PRO**	**TYPING PRO**	**TYPING PRO**
PEGGY GLENN	PEGGY GLENN	PEGGY GLENN	PEGGY GLENN
HUNTINGTON BEACH	HUNTINGTON BEACH	HUNTINGTON BEACH	HUNTINGTON BEACH
714/000-0000	714/000-0000	714/000-0000	714/000-0000
TYPING PRO	**TYPING PRO**	**TYPING PRO**	**TYPING PRO**
PEGGY GLENN	PEGGY GLENN	PEGGY GLENN	PEGGY GLENN
HUNTINGTON BEACH	HUNTINGTON BEACH	HUNTINGTON BEACH	HUNTINGTON BEACH
714/000-0000	714/000-0000	714/000-0000	714/000-0000
TYPING PRO	**TYPING PRO**	**TYPING PRO**	**TYPING PRO**
PEGGY GLENN	PEGGY GLENN	PEGGY GLENN	PEGGY GLENN
HUNTINGTON BEACH	HUNTINGTON BEACH	HUNTINGTON BEACH	HUNTINGTON BEACH
714/000-0000	714/000-0000	714/000-0000	714/000-0000
TYPING PRO	**TYPING PRO**	**TYPING PRO**	**TYPING PRO**
PEGGY GLENN	PEGGY GLENN	PEGGY GLENN	PEGGY GLENN
HUNTINGTON BEACH	HUNTINGTON BEACH	HUNTINGTON BEACH	HUNTINGTON BEACH
714/000-0000	714/000-0000	714/000-0000	714/000-0000

This version is much more effective with a border around the top to separate the important top message from the lower tear-off section. This border, as well as the press-on letters are available at most art supply shops.

(I offered them a slight discount in return for their diligence.) I placed an ad in the college newspaper. And I did such superior work that word-of-mouth advertising soon replaced my need for active advertising with the flyers. (Please permit me to brag just a little.)

STATIONERY

Unless you'll be sending out introductory letters, you may not need to invest in elaborate letterhead or envelopes just yet. If you're starting on a limited budget, you may simply type your return address on all letters. If you've hired a graphic artist to help with your business cards, though, it may be nearly as inexpensive right now to have her or him also design your letterhead and envelopes so they all coordinate. Then, when you need to use the stationery, take the artwork to a printer. Preparing the artwork is the hardest part. You can print it anytime.

*   *   *   *

Can you do any of this yourself without hiring an artist? Yes, you can. Is there an art supply store in your community? Look through the catalogs of "rub-down" and "lift-off" letters and the catalogs of special-effect graphics tapes and ready-made borders or prepared artwork. Ask for assistance from the clerk. Look through the books for ideas. Spend an afternoon letting your mind shop for ideas and graphics applications that you can do yourself. My second flyer was done entirely with materials I purchased myself. You will be amazed at the possibilities, and you'll be very proud you did it yourself.

SPECIFIC ADVERTISING

There is no way that I can tell you EVERY possible method of advertising in a specific market. I'm sure that if I tell you four ways and they work, that you can find another two or three more that will work, too.

But I will list the most obvious and the most effective methods I know. Sometimes a method for academic advertising will work in medical or legal, and vice versa. Other times a method will work in only one market. You should know YOUR market by now, and you should know yourself and your budget well enough to plan a productive advertising program.

ACADEMIC

1. Hang printed flyers in all appropriate places on college or university campuses. Look for bulletin boards near the library, bookstore, student center, cafeteria/snack bar, dormitories, etc.

2. Go to each separate department (English, Political Science, Sociology, Chemistry, Engineering, etc.) and ask the department secretary to post your flyer for the students and faculty.

3. Find the faculty lounge and ask to be allowed to post a flyer there. Many faculty members, particularly junior members, are continuing their own studies.

4. Visit the placement office, veterans' affairs office, counseling center, research librarian desk, and study labs and leave your information with someone who seems responsible enough to post it conspicuously or file it for easy reference.

5. If you are near a 4-year institution, visit the Graduate Study Office, the thesis advisor's office, and any faculty advisement centers. Leave your information there.

6. Advertise in the campus newspaper. Rates for this are unbelievably inexpensive, and the return is fantastic! Advertising once or twice a week is plenty in most cases. Faculty and students will respond to a well-written ad. I've included a few samples so you can see the variety of ways to write one.

7. Visit all the public libraries in your area and ask the reference librarian to keep your information on file. You may also be allowed to post a small sign on the community bulletin board in the library.

8. If you have an area of special expertise, send flyers to places that employ people in that subject area. Many of them will be taking classes to get ahead.

   For example: one woman's husband is a policeman and she types papers for other policemen who are getting advanced degrees to qualify for promotions. She advertises in all the police stations in her area, and she also advertises in the police association's newsletter. She is constantly busy.

   Another woman sent flyers to an engineering firm because she is an expert at typing technical/statistical papers. She received a lot of business from engineers who were going back to school for master's degrees or advanced training.

9. Visit the purchasing department of the local colleges, universities, and school districts. They frequently need temporary help to process a grant application, or to prepare a faculty member's speech or professional-journal article.

10. Visit the principal of each elementary school, junior and senior high school. Ask to have your flyer posted in a prominent place so that all the teachers will see it.

11. Visit all the private schools in your area, being sure you include any schools which employ teachers with special credentials (teachers of the deaf, teachers of emotionally disturbed children, teachers of the physically disabled). These teachers are almost always attending continuing-education classes to learn the latest developments in their fields.

Obviously, this is a lot of advertising. I suspect that one person could not do the work that would be generated by successful advertising in each of these places. But all of these options might not be available where you live. Pick out what suits your area and your skills, and then put the word out. Be prepared to be busy, and practice your most gracious "NO" speech. You'll need that speech if you did a good job on your advertising.

The particularly busy times for academic typing are: April through June and October 15th through Christmas. The only real slow time I have experienced is from July 15th until Labor Day. This time may not always be slow, either, because a lot of people are doing doctoral study or are attending off-campus programs which are in session all year long.

The slow period never caused me much of a problem, though, because I planned for it in my budget. It also coincided quite conveniently with my family's vacation plans.

BUSINESS/COMMERCIAL

1. Personally visit EVERY small business within 10 miles of your home (5 miles if you live in a heavily-developed area). Leave a 1/2-page flyer and a few business cards at each place. (My experience is that a full page gets thrown out, a 1/4 page gets lost in the file, but a 1/2 page will find a place on the bulletin board.)

An example of the kinds of places that will be glad to know about you are:

real estate offices	automobile dealers
health food stores	crafts shops
insurance brokers	travel agencies
investment firms	restaurants
accountants	small clothing stores
printers	independent grocers
designers/home decorators	

A real good trick to use in this area is to convince a small-business owner that he or she ABSOLUTELY NEEDS a mailing list or check-approval list. Offer to help compile a list in alphabetical order, using 3 x 5 cards and gummed labels. A good package-deal price for this would be $10 for each 100 names.

This would not pay you a great deal in the beginning, but the long-range effects are limitless. These small businesses will remember you when they need to send out sale notices or newsletters. They will tell their business associates about you, and they will use you to update the list periodically.

Read the literature in the library and that which is put out by the SBA that deals with advertising a small business. Become an expert at helping small businesses with their advertising by using your typing business, and you'll be in demand constantly.

2. Visit your city or town hall purchasing department. You may be a better deal than the temporary agency they've been using, especially if you have any experience at working for a municipality.

3. Obtain a listing of all the service clubs and civic organizations in your area: Kiwanis, Lions, Rotary, Chamber of Commerce, Optimist, League of Women Voters, Moose Lodge, Shriners, etc. Send their secretary and president a pleasant letter informing them of your services and sample prices.

 Make sure that this is the most beautifully perfect letter that you have ever typed. The letter should sell your professionalism and skill even more than the words you write in it.

4. Publicize your services to all your friends who are in business for themselves. Ask them to tell their associates.

5. Buy a set of magnetic signs for your car doors. When you drive around in the daytime, advertise your services. Make sure your phone number is large enough that someone can read it from a passing car.

6. Send a short letter and flyer/business card combination to all new businesses that advertise in the newspaper under "Legal Notices."

7. Use anything from the "Academic" section that might work. This could include visiting a class in mail-order sales or small-business marketing (especially one that is offered at night). These classes will probably be filled with people who would love to know about you.

 It's best to contact the instructor before you barge in on a class. Use tact and diplomacy. Try to point out to the instructor how

you can help the students with their businesses, rather than emphasizing what's in it
for you.

8. Post signs on the neighborhood bulletin
    boards of supermarkets and small neighborhood
    stores. These notices may need to be
    replaced often, but several women report a
    good supply of customers using this method.
    How popular is your local "reader board"?

9. Now that I've got your brain working, what
    more can you think of?

10. Leave a stack of business cards with every
    printer and copy shop. Many women report
    that this is one of their best referral
    sources.

MEDICAL

1. Advertise through the local medical associa-
    tion. Frequently it will provide you with
    address labels if you already have flyers or
    announcements available.

2. Visit all the medically-related offices in
    your area. This includes doctors, dentists,
    laboratories, x-ray facilities, physical
    therapists, psychologists, marriage/family
    counselors, etc. Leave a flyer and business
    card with the office manager or with the pro-
    fessional person.

3. Contact the local chapters of allied health
    professional organizations (nurses, optome-
    trists, vocational counselors, etc.). The
    work here will vary from typing meeting
    announcements, to preparing mailing lists, to
    publishing a newsletter. If there is a news-
    letter, advertise in it.

4. Contact any medical typing/transcription ser-
    vices that are already in business. Find out
    if they need help with overload. (Be sure
    you do this AFTER you have conducted your
    price survey.)

5. Use whatever fits from either of the cate-
    gories I've already discussed. Remember that

there is room for a medical-terminology background in the academic world as well.

LEGAL

1. Visit all the law offices in your area. Talk to the office manager and talk to the attorney as well. Always remember that you're out to save them both time, trouble, and money.

    My best friend is office manager for a law firm and says that her firm has two back-up typists who are absolutely indispensable in times of overload or vacations or sick leaves. She says that they would rather use these two women than go to a temporary agency for help. They are always sure of the quality of work they get from their back-up typists.

2. Advertise through the bar association by obtaining mailing labels and by inserting an ad in their newsletter or professional journal.

3. Send a flyer to any law school in your area. Ask to have it posted for students' use.

4. Also ask the law school(s) for a list of all graduating students. Send these students an announcement of your services so that they can use it once they pass the bar exam.

5. Watch the newspapers for the semi-annual listing of the names of the people who pass the bar exam. Send notices to all who live in your immediate area.

6. Contact the court-reporting services and offer your typing services. In most court-reporting firms, the stenographer is not responsible for transcribing the notes from courtroom hearings or depositions. That work is handled by a secretarial pool or by free-lance typists.

    (A little tip: I had difficulty locating these services in my Yellow Pages. I finally found them under: "Reporters, Court and Convention.")

PROFESSIONAL WRITERS

1. The current edition of WRITER'S MARKET,
    LITERARY MARKETPLACE, and THE WRITER'S HAND-
    BOOK (available at the library reference
    desk) list addresses of most writers' clubs.
    Send your flyer and business cards to the
    secretary of the clubs and ask to be invited
    to the next meeting.

2. The May issue of WRITER'S DIGEST (a magazine
    available at the library and on some news-
    stands) usually lists upcoming writer's con-
    ferences in every state. If there's a con-
    ference or meeting near you, contact the con-
    ference planner and ask to be allowed to dis-
    tribute business cards and a descriptive
    flyer during the conference. Frequently you
    can send a supply of cards and flyers and
    have them set out on a "Free - Take One" coun-
    ter. That can save you from having to sit
    through an entire conference.

3. Two writer's publications (THE WRITER and
    WRITER'S DIGEST) accept advertising from manu-
    script typists. Check a current issue of
    either publication for their different
    styles, formats, and rates.

    The advertising in these magazines is fairly
    expensive, and some women have reported good
    success while others have reported only fair
    success. It's a good idea to take just a
    little extra time before committing your
    advertising dollar.

    Write or call one of the typists who adver-
    tises in either magazine. Ask how the
    response has been to their ad. Check with
    the typists in your area first. See if the
    bulk of their work has been local people, or
    people who mail manuscripts to them. When
    asking a typist for information, please
    always enclose a stamped, self-addressed
    envelope as a courtesy.

4. LITERARY MARKET PLACE (LMP) offers free list-
    ings to typing services. Write to the pub-
    lisher, R. R. Bowker, and ask for information
    about how to be listed as a professional
    typist. (See bibliography for address.)

5. Check your local colleges for courses in pro-
    fessional writing. Contact the instructor of
    these classes and ask to be allowed to dis-
    tribute your business cards to the students.
    The potential is not overwhelming in this
    area because many writers are acceptable
    typists, and because still more of them can-
    not afford to pay someone else to type their
    work. But persevere; the market does exist!

SPECIAL CIRCUMSTANCES

As I said earlier, much of the success of your
advertising program will depend on personal contact
with potential customers. However, if you are confined
to your home either because of a disability (yours or a
family member's) or because of remote location or
because of a transportation problem, all is not lost.
As a first step, phone a school, company, office, or
writer's club. Find out to whom advertising material
should be sent. Then send your business card and a
descriptive flyer. A week later, follow up with a
phone call to assure that the material was received and
posted. If dealing by mail, be sure that each piece of
correspondence you send reflects the ultimate in per-
fection and beauty.

If you are disabled and plan to post signs on a
college campus or at community locations, ask a family
member or close friend to help you. A woman in Tampa
wrote to say that she has a post-polio friend who
maneuvers around a campus in her wheelchair holding her
flyers and tools in her lap. She takes along her teenage son who does the actual sign-posting on bulletin
boards. That's teamwork! A real family effort!

An elderly woman in the next town from me hires a
high-school girl to post her signs and run errands.
She handles the rest of her advertising by: mailing
circulars, talking on the telephone, and sending additional flyers and cards with each customer.

SUMMARY

I've just about run out of ideas (my own and those
contributed by earlier readers). Some women have written from various areas of the country to say that they
often had to make repeated contacts with some of their
early customers. Some others reported that when they

visited a business, they took along a portfolio of the work they could do. This seemed to provide good results.

What's in a portfolio? How is it presented? A portfolio should include one example of every kind of typing job you've ever done: from invoices to letters, from poetry to manuscripts, from engineering specifications to financial proposals. DO NOT INCLUDE any confidential matter that would be detrimental to a former client. Always ask permission before saving a copy for your portfolio. Purchase a 3-ring binder and some plastic or acetate sheet protectors. You'll have fun building up a portfolio. You'll be amazed at the variety of jobs you'll do, and the wide range of your skills. You should also be mighty proud when you've assembled it.

If you're just beginning, start a sample portfolio now. For introduction purposes before visiting potential clients, type a fictional letter, a fictional resume, a fictional invoice, a fictional balance sheet, a fictional term-paper page. Preparing this make-believe portfolio will also help pass the time while you're waiting for that first phone call.

If you come up with a novel advertising approach, let me know. Some of the more creative ones I've heard about were:

1. taking a half-page ad in the high-school sports program (Lots of independent-business-man-football-fathers responded to a professionally written ad in the Homecoming issue.)

2. offering to do a high school band-booster mailing list free in return for a free ad in the band's Spring concert program (The owner of a musical-instrument store hired the woman to help him keep his instrument-rental records straight.)

3. designing a "welcome letter" for an independent real estate saleswoman in exchange for having the typist's card distributed to each new home buyer and each realtor the saleswoman knew. (This produced a steady academic customer and numerous referrals.)

I believe that of the five markets I've just discussed, the most lucrative is academic. It is also the easiest in which to advertise. Keep in mind, though, that this is the case where I live. If you live in an area where very few people are attending college, or where there is already an abundance of academic typists and only a limited market, you should concentrate your skills in another market.

Use your market analysis from Chapter 3 to determine what you will do. Then use the advertising suggestions in this chapter to get the most out of your market.

I didn't list a lot of good books on advertising in this chapter,and there are plenty of them. Refer to the bibliography for more information and also visit your library or bookstore to find more that I haven't listed. I will clue you in to my favorites: **HOW TO ADVERTISE AND PROMOTE YOUR SMALL BUSINESS**, by G. M. Siegel, published by John Wiley and Sons; and **SPEAK EASY** by Sandy Livner, published by Summit Books.

CHAPTER 8
Using Publicity

AN EXPLANATION

Promotion and publicity differ from advertising in that you don't usually pay any money for publicity's end result. (You may pay to <u>implement</u> a promotion idea, but the process isn't the same as buying ad space or air time or preparing an ad brochure or card.)

By the same token, publicity makes you believable. If a story appears about you in your hometown newspaper, that's tantamount to an endorsement. By being an entrepreneur, starting a business at home as a renegade secretary, or combining the best of the work and home worlds, you've captured attention. That is news. Taking an ad in the classified section of the paper is not news. News is believable, ads are questioned. Ads aren't seen by as many people, and aren't talked about, and don't make you a celebrity.

"Publicity can take the form of news, information or actions designed to attract attention, create interest and gain support. Planning which of several forms (or routes) your publicity program will take is most important. Indeed, this is what a publicity program consists of -- different techniques working together. What can publicity do? It can:

Increase awareness of programs or services
. . . and . . .
Thereby create, build, change, or enhance a public image."

From the Publicity Handbook, © copyright by the Sperry and Hutchinson Company.

That's what it is, and why you need it. The public (your customers) will become aware of your services; and the publicity program that you design (one idea or several throughout the year) will create, build and enhance your business image in the public's mind.

To quote the Sperry booklet again, "The first step is to determine what (you) want to accomplish through a publicity program. All subsequent efforts will be based on your objectives. Set long- and short-term objectives."

"The aim of a publicity program should be to reach and influence the public (that is) important to you."

This Publicity Handbook I've quoted from is written for professional publicity directors, the folks who work to create positive public images for large corporations and organizations. But our businesses loom just as large in our own pride, don't they? Last I knew, the handbook was free for the asking. To find out if you may receive a copy, send an inquiry (please again enclose that courtesy stamped, self-addressed envelope, this time a large manila envelope with three stamps on it) to:

Sperry and Hutchinson Company
Attn: Consumer Services
2900 W. Seminary Drive
Fort Worth TX 76133

SO HOW DO YOU DO IT?

There are literally hundreds of ways to create publicity. PROMOTION creates attention, which results in PUBLICITY for what you did. I think the most logical way for me to explain this to you is to show a few examples. Here's a very clever promotion idea that generated lots of favorable publicity.

On National Secretaries' Day, one home-based typist invited all her regular clients to a light buffet lunch that she prepared. Because this was the reverse of the usual "roses and a free lunch" routine that bosses go through for their secretaries, she received coverage in her local newspaper, the radio station came out, and the local television crew stopped by for a free lunch, too.

Now then, buying the food cost her some money, preparing the food cost her a little time (which was money), and sending out invitations to the clients cost her a little time and a little money. But, consider the return on her investment. Anyone who read that day's paper, listened to the radio broadcast, or watched the television newscast knew that she was in business and that she enjoyed it. She says that she received no less than 25 new clients as a result of that one simple idea. How did she do it?

First, she thought of the idea. In an after-dinner gab session with her husband she casually mentioned how she would miss that token free lunch and bunch of roses now that she was working for herself. The next bit of conversation was about how much she appreciated the regular clients who kept her in business. That evolved into planning a small informal luncheon as a gesture of appreciation TO THEM, FROM HER. She figured she'd receive emotional roses -- the old "better to give than to receive" routine.

Second, she typed up 25 invitations to the luncheon using blank party invitations she purchased from a gift and card store. She asked for R.S.V.P.'s and 17 people said they'd show up.

Third, she told a few of her still-working friends about her party, and about how excited she was. One of those friends told her own boss who happened to tell a publicity professional at a Chamber of Commerce meeting. The publicity professional recognized a good story and called the newspaper, the radio station, and the television station (after checking with the hostess first for permission). The rest is history.

You can do the same thing, or any variation of it. If you don't have that publicity connection, do your own. Often just a telephone call will be sufficient to alert the press. How else do you suppose they find out about what's going on? Sometimes you can guarantee results by sending a written press release before, or as follow-up, to that phone call.

Again, as with much of the advertising information in the last chapter, to try and tell you everything I know about publicity, and everything there IS to know about publicity would take a whole 2-year college course and at least two or three good books, and probably 6 months' minimum of working at it. I hope, though, that with this example and more that I'll use

125

later on, you'll grasp the major points. My absolute
favorite book on publicity is:

PUBLICITY: How To Get It, by Richard O'Brien.
            Published by Harper & Row.

How does publicity work? Via the telephone, via
the typewriter, via word of mouth. The example on the
previous page is a nice idea that was turned into a
promotional event. Sometimes it's accidental, sometimes you plan it that way. Ah-ha, you're thinking
already, aren't you?

> One woman, whose business was named The
> Classical Carriage, advertised that she
> would do resumes "by appointment while
> you wait." Then, to avoid being inter-
> rupted while doing the work, she provided
> her customers with earphones and a reclin-
> ing chair so they could listen to the
> local classical radio station and relax
> for a half hour or so. Of course, not
> all customers took advantage of her
> offer, but one day the local music colum-
> nist heard about it and wrote her up in
> the Sunday paper. The manager of the
> radio station saw the item in the news-
> paper, was delighted for the unsolicited
> publicity himself, and arranged to have
> the woman's service talked about on the
> radio.

Promotion or publicity is also the use of give-
away items (freebies, trinkets, goodies) that are
printed with your company name. Pens, rulers,
refrigerator magnets, you've seen hundreds of them.
The term for these trinkets is actually "specialty
advertising items," but the effect is more of a
promotion and publicity gimmick than a real advertising
program. To find a firm that can supply you with these
items, look in the Yellow Pages under "Advertising
- Specialty."

> Another typist gave away 100 orange see-
> through plastic rulers at a church
> bazaar. Why? Her company was named
> "Golden Rule Professional Typing." And,
> of course, she had her business name
> printed on the rulers. She spent an 8-
> hour day at the bazaar and approximately
> $35 dollars on the rulers. Within a week

she had received $250 dollars' worth of
new clients. For another month, more
work poured in and she referred a lot of
it to overload helpers.

Take advantage of every possibility to tell someone (or a whole group of someones) about what you do
for a living. For instance:

Invite yourself to the high school's career day.
If the kids aren't interested, perhaps their
teachers or their parents are. The local newspaper or the school paper might also write up the
event.

If your church or synagogue has a women's group,
ask to arrange a career night where you and
several other women with interesting jobs or
businesses would give 15-20 minute presentations
about what you do.

Offer to teach a class to 4-H or Girl Scout troops
at the high-school level. Office practices or job-
finding skills or business-running skills are
popular subjects.

Whenever you attend a meeting where they perform
the "who are you-around the room-let's all tell"
ritual, be sure to sing out loud and clear just
who you are and what you do and how great it makes
you feel. This can be anything from a Tupperware
party to a PTA meeting to a meeting of the Chamber
of Commerce.

HOW OFTEN?

Why not plan one small promotion event for every
month? You can key to the various holidays or make up
excuses. For instance:

JANUARY -- "Start the new year right by having ABC
Secretarial do your resume."

FEBRUARY -- "I LOVE all my customers." Happy
Valentine's Day cards are great reminders. "I cannot
tell a lie. I'm the best there is." Washington's
Birthday hype.

MARCH -- cold? blustery? miserable? how 'bout
asking all customers to stop for a hot cup of tea when

127

they bring their work? anniversary for your business?
St. Patrick's Day party?

    APRIL -- raining? Easter eggs? Christian theme?
Passover? spring break? Secretaries' Day? first day
of Spring?

    MAY -- when was the last time you received a May
basket from a secret admirer? Could you design a "May
basket" flyer with benefits written in each flower?

    JUNE -- graduation notices for all the students
who survived? anybody getting married or celebrating
an anniversary?

    JULY -- Independence Day, the country's and
your's, too; serve iced tea to cool off those customers
who were freezing in March?

    AUGUST -- this month is yours, how 'bout a
vacation special, a back-to-school sale with 10% off
every order over $25?

    SEPTEMBER -- Labor Day, back-to-school again,
Jewish holidays

    OCTOBER -- Columbus discovered America, you
discovered the joy of self-employment and your special
clients; Halloween

    NOVEMBER -- Election Day, cast your vote for your
favorite freelance typist/secretary; Thanksgiving,
maybe a better time to send greetings than next month
when so many will be competing for attention

    DECEMBER -- snow sale? Christmas special?
Hanukkah special? end-of-the-year clearance?

    Now your mind is really whirring, isn't it? And
you thought this whole thing was so easy? It is easy!
And it's fun! And you're the boss! You're in control!

SUMMARY

    This is a short chapter, but the information
didn't seem to fit logically anywhere else. I could go
on for pages and pages, but then all you would have are
my ideas and none of your own. Besides, my brain does
run dry after a while, honest. Try to perform one

simple promotion or publicity function a week. Call up a client you haven't heard from in a while, work on a new flyer for an event or stunt next month, tell just one new person about what you do, drop a stack of business cards at just one more printer or copy shop.

The limits to a successful promotion and publicity program don't exist. There are no limits to your talent, your creativity, your drive to make a go of this. Of course, if you already have more work than you can handle, we'll forgive you. You may stay glued to the chair and keyboard until you catch up. But, as soon as it drops off, back you go to the monthly plan. No worrying or whining allowed. It doesn't fit that image you've just created. Find something to do, don't spend much money on it, but do spend some time and thought on it. And have fun!

PERSISTENCE with your PROMOTION and PUBLICITY will PRODUCE a PUBLIC image that will result in PROFITS.

*   *   *   *

P.S. Whatever positive publicity you receive is positive publicity for the whole profession -- for everyone else who works at home with a typewriter or word processor, for every secretary everywhere. Publicity and promotion are ways to get the world to stand up and recognize that there is great dignity in working with words, a keyboard, and paper.

We're artists. It takes a special skill to turn out a clean manuscript, a crisp letter with uniform margins and balance on the page, a financial proposal with straight columns, a commanding resume that helps someone land a new job. We have that skill and we want everyone to know it, respect us for it, and pay us well for it.

Please.
Thank you.
You're welcome.

How soon?   How much?

CHAPTER 9

Effective Customer Strategies

A home-based typing business depends upon customers. A SUCCESSFUL home-based typing business depends upon EFFECTIVE CUSTOMER RELATIONS -- public relations.

Businesses lose customers primarily because of personality conflicts or emotional reasons -- not because of poor workmanship. Most businesses don't do shoddy work. Getting along with your customers, and making sure they get along with you requires some pre-planning.

The time to decide on your business' general policies and procedures is now, before you have to "think on your feet." What is your policy on deposits for large orders, on checks or cash, on who fixes errors, on being asked to do something that may be unethical or illegal?

The time to decide how to handle a crisis is NOW, before it happens. Anticipate every situation you can imagine and have a plan ready. That's the difference between being an employee and being in charge. You are the planner, you are the one who copes.

ON THE PHONE

There are many areas to consider here. I'll start from the minute a customer calls to inquire about your work, your prices, deadlines, etc., and I'll go through all the processes. I think the easiest way to illustrate my points so that you understand what I mean is for me to give you guidelines based on my experience, and sprinkle in conversation examples.

First decide how you will answer your telephone.
On page 102 we talked about this a little bit. First
you smile and are cheerful. Then you figure out what
to say. It can be as simple as "hello," or as complicated as "Good afternoon, Sandy's Secretarial Service.
How may I help you?"

In my academic business, I preferred "hello." I
didn't have a separate phone line for my business, and
I never knew if a caller was for my business or for one
of the kids or for my husband. I felt it was presump-
tious of me to answer the only phone in the house by
saying, "Hello, Peggy Glenn, professional typist."

However, if you have a separate line installed in
your home, and if you operate with a fictitious business name, then by all means answer that telephone line
with your company name. As already discussed on page
90, when deciding on a company name, consider how easy
it will be to say when answering the phone. A real
tongue-twister can be embarrassing, and may be a
drawback.

I think there is an advantage to this set-up if
you will be typing for businesses; that is, if you
specialize in business typing. Somehow you'll have
more identification and credibility in the business
world if you are "Pat's Secretarial Service" or
"Terri's Typing" than if you are just another "hello"
on the end of the line. There again, and I know you're
probably tired of reading it by now but it's the truth,
YOU know your customers. You know yourself. Don't
take my word as THE word. Use that mind of your own.

Once you've figured out how to answer the phone,
always be sure that you get a customer's name and
telephone number as soon as you have any formal contact. If you don't catch the name the first time, ask
again in the middle of the conversation. People enjoy
being addressed by name. The difference between anony-
mity and reality is their name. When the call is completed, address her or him by name and say, "Thank you,
Ann, I'll be looking forward to our 3 o'clock appointment."

Why the number? If you have set up an appointment, for example, you may need to be able to get in
touch with him or her if you have an emergency and must
reschedule the appointment. In addition, once you have
the customer's work, having the phone number will
enable you to call to check on any discrepancies (words

left out, words you can't read, something that doesn't make sense, etc.).

After you have finished typing for that customer, jot his or her number on a 3 x 5 file card and keep it handy. In the beginning it is nice to call customers every few months and remind them that you enjoyed typing for them and are available if they need more work done. You can also thank them for any referrals they have sent. That's an extension of both the advertising and publicity lessons from the previous chapters.

If they have mentioned a possible deadline, and you haven't received the work yet, reminding them that it is approaching may be just the memory-jog they need to get working on the paper and get you to type it.

As an another example of good P.R. (public relations) and good record-keeping, suppose that Customer "A" is a computer expert, and Customer "B" just happens to need someone to write a program for his bill collecting. Offer to put the two of them together. Maintain confidentiality while arranging this meeting, however. You mention to Customer B that you have a possible solution for his problem because you know of Customer A. You "know of" customer A, you don't work for him. Carry through that way, and if both parties agree to be contacted, then give away both phone numbers.

As another example, if Customer "Y" makes hand-painted beer mugs and you need one for a gift, you'll have your own personal Yellow Pages.

BEFORE

NEVER, NEVER, NEVER commit yourself to a price quote or a time quote on the telephone without first seeing the work. You can quote your hourly or per/page prices, but don't quote a finished price or a definite deadline.

One of the most uncomfortable experiences I had was when I'd been in business for about 2 weeks. A man called at 10 a.m. and said he had ten pages of typing that he needed for a meeting the next morning. Because my specialty is academic typing, I assumed he meant double-spaced typing. For some stupid reason I also assumed I'd be typing from handwritten or rough-typed copy.

As it turned out, he was a real estate salesman who had seen my ad on a college bulletin board. He assumed I was a student and that he could get cheap labor and demand a lot.

When he arrived, the ten pages were to be done single-spaced in elite type with only a 3/4 inch margin on the left, and half an inch on the top, right, and bottom. That's approximately four times as much work as is on a page of double-spaced pica typing with standard academic margins.

The copy I was to type from was also single-spaced with numerous scratch-outs, write-overs, and inserts on separate slips of paper that were attached in no particular order. I had to hunt for each insert among the miscellaneous scraps.

To make matters worse, I had told him on the phone that the job would cost him about $10 or $12 and that I could get it done by early evening. (That was when I first started and I gave almost every customer same-day or next-day service.)

The clock chimed noon, and I swallowed hard at having been so naive. I almost pushed him out the door so I could get started right away. I knew the afternoon was going to be too short for what I had to do.

He couldn't have driven five blocks when he stopped at a pay phone and called me with a correction that he had forgotten. During the rest of the afternoon he called me six more times with corrections -- two of them were corrections to the corrections. I had to type four pages over, and by 5 o'clock I was a wreck!

I finally took the phone off the hook so that I could finish the job. He was supposed to pick it up at 6:30. He showed up at 7:15 and was very angry that the phone had been busy and that he hadn't been able to give me two more corrections!

I mumbled something about teenagers on the phone and numbly took the $10 he shoved at me. I knew good and well that the job was worth at least $40, and at that time I couldn't afford to be duped out of $30. Right then and there I made up my mind that I'd never type for him again. I also promised myself never to commit myself on the phone for a deadline or finished price. BUT, I held my cool. I thanked him for his business, and gave him my card. The old "service with a smile and clenched teeth" routine.

Believe it or not, he called me about two weeks later and asked if I were free to do some more work for him. We were having tuna sandwiches for supper and the menu for the rest of the week was dismal, but I decided that HE wasn't worth it!

Here's the line I gave him.

"Oh, Mr. Johnson, how nice to hear from you. I'm so sorry! I just this morning took on a job that will keep me booked through next Wednesday. I wish I could type for you. Can I help you find another typist? I'm sure if you call the colleges or secretarial services in the Yellow Pages you can find someone to help you right away. I know your work is important and demands immediate attention."

Now, I ask you! Is that a line? And I delivered it without busting out in laughter or being struck by lightning for lying through my teeth. I wasn't sicky sweet, either. But he thinks I was really impressed by his C-R-A-P. I'll tell you what, though -- over the next 2 years I never typed for him again, but he sent me over $400 worth of business via referrals from folks he knew. He told them all how gracious I was, how I went out of my way to help him when I couldn't do his work.

Mind you, when I referred him to another service, I chose one that operated in an office and charged more because of their overhead. Then I alerted the other service and they dealt with him before he could cause them any grief. In truth, they were better equipped to handle his needs. There were three typists and a manager who could put the "power" on one of his jobs if he needed it. He also had to schedule appointments, and they made sure he paid a premium if he was late bringing in the work. His work was "business" and I enjoyed "academic." We were all happy. That's that networking and referral I talked about in the very first chapter. There's more about it later.

*   *   *   *

Since then I've never been badgered into a phone quote for prices or deadlines. Here's a typical initial phone conversation with a customer. My "lines" are in the bold type, the "customer" talks in regular type.

"Hello, I'm calling about typing. Is this Peggy Glenn?"

"Yes, speaking. How can I help you?"

"Well, I have a little term paper that I need to have typed. Can you do it and how much will it cost me?"

"First I need to know how long it is, what shape it's in right now, and when you need it."

"We-e-e-l-l-l-l, the teacher said it was supposed to be about 14 pages, I'm not finished writing it, and it's due Friday."

"That may be a problem; this is Wednesday. Does the paper have footnotes or tables? Do you need help with spelling, grammar, or punctuation?"

"Yeah, it'll need a little fixing up. And the teacher said it was up to us if we used footnotes; but it has to have a bibliography. Do you know what that

136

is? What I really need to know, though, is how much it's gonna cost me."

"My rates are $10 an hour or a minimum of $1.50 per double-spaced page depending on what I'm typing from and what the finished product will be. I type 90 words-a-minute, but if I can't read it, or if it is technical material, I can't go that fast."

"Oh." (long pause) "Well, do you think I can get out of it for less than $15?"

"That'll depend entirely on how well I can read what you give me, if you get it here in time for me to do it, how many pages it ends up being, and how much I have to fix it up."

"You mean you can't tell me for sure that it won't cost me more than $15?"

"That's right! I can't be sure until I see your work. I don't want to mislead you and then surprise you when you come to pick up the work. I'll be happy to give you an estimate before I type it, but I can't tell you anything more until I actually see the work."

"O.K. Well, I'll finish it up this afternoon and bring it to you in the morning. Is that okay?"

"Yes, the morning will be all right, but I _have_ to have it by 10 o'clock if I'm expected to give it _back_ to you for a Friday morning class. I need the whole day to type it, and I want to proofread it again Friday morning before you pick it up. This time there will be no RUSH charge, but in the future, if I have less than 2 days, I charge time-and-a-half. It's for your own protection. If I have to rush on a job, I run the risk of making errors, and that's not fair to you. That's not what you pay for. I hope you understand."

Always make _them_ responsible for the decisions. Try to let them know that you have _their_ best interest at heart. You don't want your customers to think that you are a mercenary who lays in wait for poor innocents. You want them to think that their work is THE most important piece You will handle that day. That they really count with you!

You can't always size up the customers on the phone. Sometimes the most polished and sincere-sounding customer on the phone turns out to be a real ogre

STATEMENT

PEGGY GLENN
PROFESSIONAL TYPIST

⌐.

#1 Crabby Customer

School of Unpleasantness

⌐   ⌐

XXDXXXXXXXXXXXXX XXXXXXXXXXXXXXXXXXXXXXXXXXXXXXXXXXXXXXXXXXXXXXXXXXXXXX.

Date	Description	Amount
1/7	Consultation regarding typing 1 hour	$7.00
1/8	Typing--12 pages @ $1.25	15.00
	6 phone calls @ 15 min/each (90 min @ $7/hr)	10.50
	Call to library to check incomplete reference--30 min.	3.50
1/9	Corrections to 8 pages to correct customer's error (retyping necessary)	10.00
1/9	Additional phone calls--30 min.	3.50
		$49.50

Thank you for your business. Be sure to recommend me
to your friends who need accurate and thorough work by
a PROFESSIONAL.   Peggy Glenn

PAID BY CHECK NO.

8K 884 Rediform

once you are working on the paper, or when he or she comes to pick up the work.

In my business, the majority of the difficult customers were male. I think it's because they were so used to categorizing women as subservient. In spite of my best efforts, to some of them I was still "just a secretary." They didn't view me as an equal -- as a professional -- until they received my bill. In all fairness to the male of the species, however, nearly all my customers were pleasant. My point here is that of the few who were difficult, the majority of them were male.

In my experience, women have been more tolerant and more accepting of me as an equal partner in the production of a quality typewritten document. They are the writers, and I am the polisher. It's kind of like the collaboration of cookbook author and experienced cook who can work as a team, or design artist and production engineer.

DURING

DON'T PUT UP WITH rudeness, disrespect, or needless interruptions. Make them pay for their ill manners or arrogance.

I once knew a traffic officer who said that the more belligerent a person became, the more he "stuck it to 'em" with his pencil and citation book. The same principle can be applied in the home-based typing business. The more arrogant a customer is -- the more he or she interrupts you, or the more you have to go out of your way to fix up the work you're doing without any appreciation from them -- the more times you hit the "add" key on the calculator.

An itemized invoice or bill is the best way to persuade this kind of customer that you are above that sort of treatment. I've included one here for you to see exactly what I mean.

Sometimes when I get an over-anxious customer who just seems to have a case of the jitters and isn't sure you're going to be finished with his or her work, I simply avoid answering the phone. I turn on my answering device and put a message on it that says something like:

Thank you for calling. Right now I'm
tied up with a very important typing project for a special customer. I must pay
close attention to what I'm doing to
avoid errors. I appreciate your understanding. At the sound of the tone,
please leave your name and number, and
I'll call back as soon as possible.

That is usually enough to humble the most arrogant
customer, and ease the fears of the ones who worry too
much. At the same time, I can monitor the incoming
calls. If I hear a message that I must answer, I simply cut in on the machine. My family is used to it,
too. Their standard message is, "Mom, are you there?"
If I am really not at home, they usually leave a message. It's become a joke around here: "Mom, are you
there?"

*   *   *   *

ALWAYS PROOFREAD your work one more time before
the customer arrives.

I always allowed myself one extra day on the deadline just for proofreading. I usually put the work
away for the night and proofread it first thing the
next morning when my brain was fresh. Many times I
picked up a small error that could be fixed in no time
at all, but which would probably would have irritated
the customer, especially if the work were being turned
in to an important class. Whether it's academic,
medical, legal, business, or for writers, it's supposed
to be correct.

(I hope there aren't any errors in this book.
It's been proofread by at least 4 people, and not all
of them caught all the same errors. If you find one,
please just forgive me and them. We did our very best.
Please don't write me letters about them. You know
I'll find them myself the week after this comes from
the printer, and I'll be embarrassed enough already.)

Here's one of the easiest methods: use a ruler
and a soft pencil. Read the work aloud to be sure
there are no words left out. By having to say the
words, there is a better chance of catching errors.
When you find a mistake, mark a small "x" lightly in
the margin opposite the line that contains the error.
By not marking in the text, you eliminate having to
retype the whole page.

So what happens if you've proofread, found no
errors, and one shows up later (either you missed it or
the customer's copy was wrong to start with). My
standard policy for "who pays for mistakes" was: If
the error was mine (word or phrase left out, words
repeated, typographical errors, pages numbered wrong,
etc.), I redid the work or repaired the mistakes at
absolutely no charge to the customer.

However, if the customer had left out a vital part
of the work, or the handwriting was illegible, I
charged for redoing any pages necessary. This is only
fair.

Sometimes when you're extremely busy, or when
you've typed more than one draft of a paper, you might
want to hire someone else to do the proofreading. I
had very good luck with a retired schoolteacher. She
was overjoyed to be needed, she enjoyed reading college
or university papers, and she paid close attention to
every detail. She picked up such small things as dupli-
cate page numbers, missing page numbers, and dates that
didn't correspond in separate sections of a thesis.
She also caught it when I forgot to close a quotation.

She charged me only about 7¢ a page to have her
take the responsibility for proofreading, and my
customers really appreciated the added time and effort
I took with their work. It's another of those small
extras that can make a home-based typing business look
so professional!

*   *   *   *

ALWAYS MEET YOUR DEADLINES if humanly possible.
If there is the slightest possibility that you will be
unable to meet a customer's deadline, call the customer
immediately and explain your circumstances. The sooner
you let the customer know, the more likely it is that
you'll be forgiven...and the sooner the customer can
make her or his own arrangements for the delay.

I had to back out just once. I called the woman
about 3 days in advance to tell her that I was sick
with the flu and wasn't positive that I could meet her
deadline. I offered to find another typist to help me,
I offered to call her instructor, and I offered to give
her the completed part of the paper to prove to the
instructor that the delay was my fault and not hers.
You know how often a professor hears, "My typist didn't
finish it yet."

My customer was absolutely great to me in return!
She said that I didn't need to worry, that she would
call her instructor right away and explain the circumstances and that if her instructor had a problem, she
(the customer) would take it up with the dean. This
was her last paper of the semester and all of her other
papers had been turned in on time.

I didn't expect that kind of response from my customer, but it was clear she was in my corner. She
quickly reassured me and then told me to get lots of
rest, take two aspirin, and call her when I was done
with her paper. Familiar advice with an unfamiliar
refrain.

That kind of rapport is necessary with customers,
especially repeaters. You can establish that rapport
by being honest and reliable with your customers from
the beginning. I value that sort of relationship
almost more than I value the money. That is the kind
of mutual respect that I never had in a job. But I
have it now in my business and it is very, very nice.
That's another one of the many ways in which I measure
my "success."

*   *   *   *

PAY ATTENTION TO SMALL DETAILS. Whenever you can
improve on a customer's work by correcting spelling,
rearranging awkward sentences, fixing punctuation,
etc., do it. If you catch an error in addition, or any
mathematical equation, check with the customer and then
put in the correct number(s).

This thoroughness and personalized touch will make
you a valuable asset to your customers. This is one of
the reasons they will be willing to pay you well.
Being conscientious and careful isn't quite enough,
though. You also have to tell them about it. Point
out where you put forth extra effort, where you fixed
errors, where you improved. They need to know it.

If you haven't been able to justify a high price
in the beginning, as soon as you get a supply of steady
customers, you can raise your prices gradually and
they'll never ever complain. If they do, they probably
aren't worth your talents. That may sound crude and
egotistical, but if you think highly of yourself, so
will your customers. If you don't, they won't, and
you'll never receive the respect you deserve nor be
paid the price you deserve.

One other feature I have for regular customers is the "absent drop-off and pick-up." If I'm not home, they are free to put their work through a slot in my front door. If I must leave the house before they are able to pick up their work, I sometimes enclose the finished work in an envelope that I attach to the front door. They simply pick up their work and leave my money or check in the mail slot which drops directly into the house.

I do this ONLY with regular customers. I don't want strangers slipping things through my door slot, and I don't want to broadcast about when I'll be away from home. When setting up appointments I sometimes tell little white lies to guarantee my free time.

> I'm sorry, but I can't see you until 6:30 p.m. I have customers in the morning and afternoon, and would prefer to schedule you for an appointment after I've finished eating my dinner.

What I didn't say was that I was going shopping with a friend in the morning, and had an appointment with the orthodontist in the afternoon. I had already made those plans, but didn't want to advertise that no one would be home. Nor did I want to cancel my shopping trip. Everyone deserves a little break now and then. (I also turn on the answering machine so people think I'm hard at work.) Ah-h-h, the luxuries of self-employment and self-regulation of one's schedule.

AFTER

DON'T TAKE CHECKS from a customer on the first visit (unless that customer is a business or you feel the customer would be grossly offended, and why would an honest customer take offense).

Again, I got burned once. My now-standard pitch is:

> I prefer not to take checks until I have established a business relationship with you. I had one unpleasant experience trying to collect on a bad check, and I'd rather not have an adversary

association with you. I'd be happy to
give you a receipt for tax purposes, but
until I have typed for you on a more
regular basis, I'm sure you can honor my
policy of cash.

That speech works like a charm. No one has
refused to pay me, and no one has been uncomfortable
about paying me in cash. Of course, I tell them this
when they _first_ leave the work with me; sometimes I
tell them on the telephone before the appointment in
case the job is large and I would need to require a
deposit. It would be pretty embarrassing to have to
make a customer come back another time.

Now, obviously, if you type for well-established
businesses or professional people, you can't always
follow that rule. Occasionally you must be flexible.
But it is imperative that you stick to it when dealing
with individuals. There is no guarantee that you will
see them again. And once they have the finished
typed product, what's to stop them from
disappearing from your life forever?
Cash-and-carry -- it's been the way in
our country since the days of the
Pilgrims.

By the same token, don't give back
the work if the customer shows up without
cash or checkbook. In this case I don't
mind asking the customer to make a second
trip. They understood right from the
start what my policy was regarding payment.
The only time I make allowances is when I've been
typing for a customer on a regular basis for several
months. Then occasionally I've been known to "slide"
them until payday if they forgot or were "short."

*   *   *   *

KEEP IN TOUCH with the pleasant customers. As I
mentioned on the second page of this chapter, a good
rapport between you and your customers is an invaluable
business asset.

Keep a 3 x 5 card file (or an address book) with
all your customers' names, phone numbers, and
addresses. You never know when you might need to contact one of them. If you deal with business or professional customers, you might consider sending them holi-
day greeting cards in November or December.

As I mentioned earlier, don't hesitate to contact a customer if you feel you can offer assistance in his or her subject area (or if you need information that one of them might have). This is how the "good old boy" networks get started.

You can develop a reliable resource list in a short time. After only about a year, my pile of 3 x 5 cards had outgrown the rubber band and graduated to one of those plastic boxes with A-Z dividers. Occasionally I review the file to update addresses and phone numbers. I rarely throw out a card, but I have been known to part with some if I didn't hear from the customer for over a year. This will be up to you.

ETHICS

Confidentiality, how much "editing" is fair for college students," what to do when asked to plagiarize, what to do when asked to alter a document, what to do when asked to do a "little investigative letter-writing and phone calling." You don't think it'll happen? It may not, but then again it may. Give some thought to these issues now and be prepared to stand your ground without compromise. Each of you will deal with these issues differently.

CONFIDENTIALITY. Consider this scenario:

A customer brings you a resume, and that customer is obviously already employed in one position but is seeking employment somewhere else. She leaves you a telephone number. You finish the resume early and call her up. She's not at her desk, so you leave the following message with a clerk: "This is ABC Secretarial. Please tell Joanie that her new resume is finished."

Whoa! Now at least one person at her present job knows that Joanie is having her resume redone; whether she wants them to know is another story. They don't know if she's trying for an internal promotion or if Joanie is looking around for a new position. You've seriously compromised your confidentiality with customer, Joanie. But be open about it. If you've made such a serious error, try to reach her again to tell her about it immediately so that she can cover her tracks -- if it isn't too late.

Here's another example. Suppose one of your clients is a private investigator or a psychologist or an investigative reporter who is working on a "hot book"? In any of these instances, and in many more, you'll be typing or transcribing material which must be kept in the strictest confidence. Acknowledge and accept this responsibility, and you'll always have plenty of work. Betray this confidentiality, and your business is doomed.

EDITING FOR COLLEGE STUDENTS.

When do you draw the line? When is it cheating for you to rewrite a customer's work, particularly a student? When is it acceptable? Here's how I handled it. If my thinking helps you form your policy, I'm pleased. This is a difficult one for many folks, and I hope I can help you through it.

The bulk of my typing business was academic, and the majority of that work was performing minor and/or major editing for my clients. Depending on the client, I applied one of several standards. For a beginning freshman student, I would not perform anything but very minor spelling, punctuation, and verb/subject agreement editing. I figured that someone fresh from high school (and I talk here of the young freshman rather than someone returning to school after years of working) would only continue to be deluded about his/her lack of skills if someone like me fixed it up time and time again before it was turned into the instructor.

I also found out, much to my complete dismay, that many of the teachers didn't know what was correct, and beyond that, that they didn't care if the student per-formed well grammatically as long as a paper came in and as long as the paper presented good ideas in a logical format.

On the other hand, a lot of my clients were people who had been working for as many as 20 years at a vocation, i.e., nurses, firemen, policemen. In many cases, training for these jobs 15-20 years ago was not academic, but rather vocational. And some of them had received no formal college schooling at all, only on-the-job training.

In order to advance (and sometimes to stay afloat) in their field, these people now needed to obtain at least a bachelor's degree, and some tried desperately for a master's degree. Often they were still working full time while attending accelerated-pace programs at off-site campus locations. In addition to this brutal schedule, many of them were handicapped further. Most of these clients were locked into the jargon of their professions; most of them didn't know correct written sentence structure. Their vocabulary was pitifully shallow.

They were paying me as a consultant, as a translator -- I changed their words from jargon into academese. I was proud and not offended to provide extensive editing and in some cases rewriting for these clients. I rationalized that businesses employ professional writers and editors for this very function. I saw my work as an extension of my clients' business efforts, rather than as an attempt to subvert the educational process.

In between the 19-year-old freshman and the 45-year-old freshman were all kinds of other clients. I used a variety of editing skills to meet their needs and still satisfy my conscience.

PLAGIARIZE.

I couldn't. First, I'm a writer by profession, was a writer then, when I was typing. I couldn't. For me it was personal, and not a matter of professional ethics. Second, I'd been a student and worked hard for my grades, struggled with research, written rough drafts and edited drafts. Third, I'd been a secretary to college and university professors, and I didn't like the idea of some student passing a fast one on a professor. Here again, running your own business allows you to make decisions and justify them. Refusing to accept work from a client is a lot different from refusing to do work for a supervisor. In the first instance, it's okay. In the second, you'd be fired.

However, I've talked with dozens of other typists whose policy is, "We'll type anything. It's not our position to judge." I don't argue with their decision. I don't think they're wrong. I couldn't do it, but that doesn't make it wrong. Decide in your own mind how you feel about this issue and have your speech prepared (or none if you don't need one) when the first college student brings a paper to you that he or she is copying from the library or has purchased from a term-paper broker.

ALTERING A LEGAL OR IMPORTANT DOCUMENT.

For many of the same emotional and philosophical reasons, I refused this kind of work, also. I'm not sure if I could have been held criminally liable (an attorney might have had to prove that I was aware of what I was doing if I had done it), but I didn't want to take the chance and I couldn't morally or ethically do it. I almost was assaulted over that one. I guess my "No" speech was a little defensive or a little preachy. If it hadn't been for my dog and my screen door, I'd have been in trouble, I think.

INVESTIGATING, SNOOPING.

I felt that if a customer wanted me to make telephone inquiries or send letters of inquiry, then that customer should be willing to pay me the going rate for a private investigator. However, I didn't have the courage to come right out and say this, so I simply said I was too busy.

WHAT ELSE COULD GO WRONG?

You could be asked to type letters that you know contain lies. For example, a worker's compensation appeal letter from a man who claims an incapacitating back injury, but who drops off the work while on his way to participate in a bowling tournament. For another example, a woman who is receiving generous financial support from "a friend" while applying for a college loan to the disadvantaged.

A foreign student who can barely read your ad brings you a paper that is obviously written by someone else. Will you type it?

But this was the kicker for me? How would you have reacted?

I had been typing for Mr. X for almost 2 years. He was attending college nights in addition to his regular job. Either Mr. X or his messenger would deliver and pick up the work. Within weeks after his graduation, I received a call from a woman who identified herself as Mrs. X. It seems that Mr. X and his messenger were "very close friends," and now Mrs. X

148

wanted to know the name, address, phone
number, and vital statistics on the messenger. I didn't know, and hadn't paid
attention since she had always been identified as "the messenger" and I naively
thought that was her only function. I
knew nothing and was, for once, grateful
for my ignorance.

If I had known, if I had been privy to the situation, how should I have handled the telephone call from
Mrs. X? I realize that hindsight is always much
sharper than foresight, but I think I'd have played
ignorant even if I hadn't been. Why? Mainly because
I'm too selfish to have allowed my valuable typing time
(MONEY-MAKING time, remember) to be caught up in a
court case. Secondarily, my business was typing, and I
preferred to keep all client contacts confidential.

You'll have a "kicker," too. Suppose a presiden-
tial advisor showed up at your door with a confidential
memo. When they travel, who do you suppose does their
typing? Suppose, suppose, suppose -- anything's
possible. Be confidential, be professional, and be
paid well.

SUMMARY

I don't know where I got my glib tongue or where I
came up with all those snazzy-sounding things to say.
My father says it's Irish malarkey, and my husband has
another word for it (expletive deleted). I call it
customer management with a little of the feminine survival instinct thrown in for good measure. You call it
whatever you choose -- as long as it works for you.

If you hold your temper, conduct yourself as a professional businesswoman, plan ahead for all sorts of
unusual or out of the ordinary occurrences, and stick
to the few basic guidelines I've presented here, you'll
be happy and successful.

When I make my customers feel important (even when
they are obnoxious or insignificant), when I make them
see me as a real pro (even if I'm maybe still an
amateur), when they know I'll respect their need for
privacy and confidentiality, and when I get them off my
back so I can enjoy my business -- then I've accom-
plished what I set out to do. I'm running my business;
it's not running me.

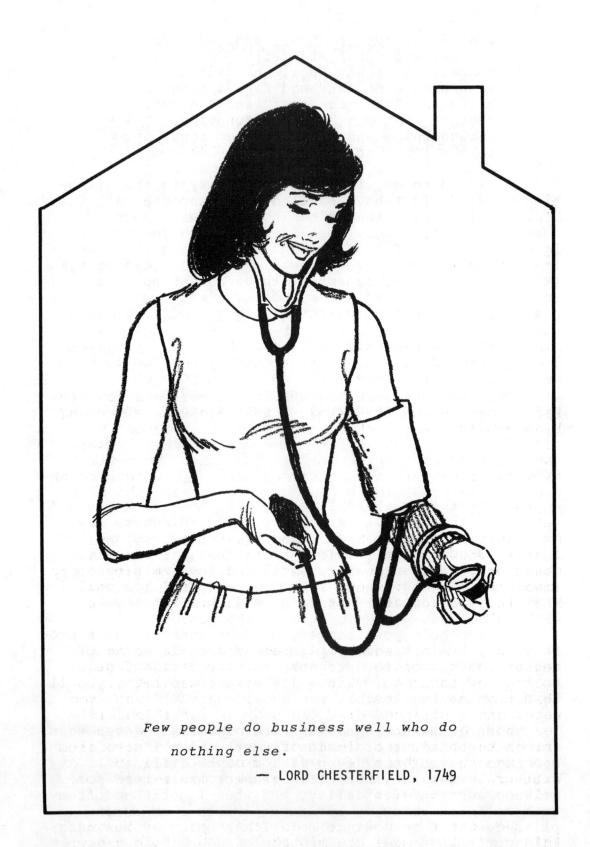

Few people do business well who do
nothing else.
— LORD CHESTERFIELD, 1749

CHAPTER 10
Take Care of Yourself

The biggest investment in your home-based typing business is YOU. You are far more valuable than any piece of equipment you can buy, rent, lease, or borrow. Without YOU, none of that equipment can operate.

Imagine that your body is the latest in automotive technology -- one of a kind -- only highly-trained and highly-paid specialists can work on it. You can't afford to have that body break down, and your budget can't afford any repair bills. Unplanned "down-time" is minus-revenue; and replacement parts (bionics, transplants) are still in the experimental stage (which is scientific talk for very expensive!).

Just as every school teacher has told you, and just as you hear on TV and read in the best women's magazines, diet, exercise, rest, and fun are very, very important. What you put into your body and how you keep it in shape will determine what kind of job it will do for you when you need it the most.

Now, I'm not advocating that you stock up on health foods, become a vegetarian, or abstain from alcohol or tobacco. That's not what I mean at all. What I am saying is that you should eat ONLY what you need, eat a balanced diet (as best as inflation will let you), get exercise other than pounding the typewriter keyboard, get plenty of rest, and plan recreation and fun. These few basic common-sense guidelines will truly make a difference in how trouble-free your self-employment will be.

How can I be so sure? How can I preach to you this way? I've made the mistake of too little exercise

and too little rest and too little fun. The mistake
cost me time away from work, cost me money for medical
bills, and caused significant disruption in my personal
life. Would you ever think it was possible to hate the
sight and sound of a typewriter? Pound on it for 12 or
14 hours a day, for too many days in a row, and see?
You'll hate it and so will everyone around you.

DENNIS the MENACE

"I DIDN'T MEAN TO EAT IT ALL UP...BUT THE PART THAT
WAS LEFT KEPT GETTIN' SMALLER AN' SMALLER, TILL IT WAS
HARDLY WORTH SAVIN'."

DIET

You have all learned about the basic 4 food
groups. Meat, Dairy, Cereal, and Vegetable/Fruit.
That's grade school stuff. What you might also do is
look through your favorite cookbook and take note of
the foods you normally eat which are highest in calories. Eliminate some of them from your diet because
you won't need as many calories once you sit in the
typing chair for more than a week.

Substitute those high-calorie munchies for some with fewer calories and maybe more food value. After 3 years I can finally pass up salted cashews for a juicy, ice-cold apple, but I still have trouble eating celery in place of Oreos and a nice cold glass of milk.

Maybe my strategy will work for you. The one sure way for me to eat less is simply to buy and cook less. If the food doesn't appear on the table, I can't eat it. I hate putting away the leftovers, and I also hate to throw things away, so I always used to eat them instead. The large economy size food doesn't really save me money if I have to buy new large economy-size clothes.

If you've been working at an outside job before starting your typing business, you will probably start to put on weight right through the sitting part of your once-beautiful body. There is a strong tendency for home-based typists to walk less and less because now even the walk from the bus stop, subway station, or parking lot has been eliminated. With a home-based business, you walk only from room to room.

Consequently, muscles get soft, and the calories taken in are more than those expended. The dial or numbers on the scales go up as does the size of the clothes in your wardrobe, and also the potential for health problems. I'm no one to talk, I've made the mistakes. And I'm trying to undo them still.

If you haven't been used to working outside the home, and you start a busines on top of your household job, you may find much the same problem. Typing doesn't expend the same energy that pushing a vacuum does, and you will probably push the vacuum less frequently anyway once you start your business. So, you simply require less to eat UNLESS you do something else to use up those unexpended calories. Read later on in the exercise and fun sections.

Suppose you intend to use your typing business as extra income -- that is, in addition to a "real job" in the "real world." In this instance, you may face the problem of eating poorly because you will be pushed for time and will grab for junk foods and convenience foods in an effort to have more time to type. All I can say is, please, use caution. Keep a mental note of what you are eating. When you start to feel plump around the edges or sluggish and irritable, look to your diet as a possible part of the reason.

EXERCISE

All of that stuff I just said about watching your food applies equally to watching your exercise level. Weight-gain is a significant and very obvious result of too little exercise. In addition, lack of exercise and toning can mean that you'll push your body beyond its limits. This phenomenon sneaks up on you, though. And curing the problem takes almost as long as getting the problem. That time will cost you money.

The muscles of the upper and lower back, neck, and arms must be conditioned and kept in shape if they are to give you the best service. Muscles which are not kept in shape become fatigued and subject to injury.

Typing is an almost constant isometric exercise. Too much of it is disastrous. If you're a little skeptical, or if you believe me but don't know exactly what I mean, do this:

Sit in a chair or stand up. Place your elbows even with your waistline, and not quite touching your body. Bend your arm 90° at the elbow, so that your forearm is parallel to the floor. Now, wiggle your fingers for 10 minutes. Feel the strain? Wiggle them for another 10 minutes. Don't move your elbows, don't move your wrists, don't move your shoulders. Simply hold your arms still and wiggle your fingers.

Yes, now maybe you can see how hours and hours of this a day with no break, with no conditioning, can set you up for pain, discomfort, and very real injury. To avoid the intrusion of this pain and injury, do something else with your body to keep it in shape and to relieve the tension of constant typing (the mental tension as well as the muscle tension).

I'm not saying that you have to lift weights or train as much as an athlete does; but you must do something to keep in shape, and you should do it every day. Check with your doctor before you start, so that you don't exceed your cardiac or respiratory limits. Also check with an exercise specialist for what's best for you. Explain how you use your arms. He or she will be able to develop a set of very simple exercises that will keep you in shape to do the job. Once you start on a program, stick to it. Make as much of a commitment to your health as you do to your business.

What can you do for exercise? There are a lot of alternatives. Probably the least expensive (and least embarrassing if you tend to shy away from parading your body in a leotard) is to tune in the television set to a show that calls for at-home participation in a carefully planned exercise program. As far as I can find out, nearly every area of the country has at least one such show in its daily repertoire. As I write this, Richard Simmons is the current rage.

Another nearly free alternative is a daily walk. Perhaps you can walk to the bank each day with the money you made the previous day. Walking has mental health benefits as well as fitness benefits. Half an hour's walk in the fresh air is supposed to be good for clearing the mind and relieving tension. That's what all the experts in the magazines say, anyway.

I love my walk. It's nearly the only time of the day I can call my own. There are no phone interruptions and I feel like a new person when I come home after half an hour. I always take a different route, and I bet I can tell you every home within 5 miles of me that has a barking dog, needs a roof repaired, could use a coat of paint. You'd also be surprised how many decorating and landscaping ideas I wish I had time and money to implement. Oh, well, one of these days. Daydreaming is fun.

I also ride my bike when I have to travel any distance or have light shopping to do. I use my bicycle when I'm especially tired or have been working unusually hard on a project. I seem to unwind more on my bike than I do on foot.

Tennis, running, swimming, skiing, rollerskating, and dancing are popular in different parts of the country. These activities also burn up lots of calories as well as providing good exercise. The latest booklet from the President's Council on Physical Fitness has a complete list of calories expended in these activities.

To get a copy of this booklet, send 60¢, your name and address, and specify booket 121H to:

Consumer Information Center
Pueblo, Colorado 81009

If you have the money and the time, you can join a health club, exercise spa, or even sign up for a bowling league. Whatever you like to do best, DO IT. No cheating, though, you're the only one who will suffer.

Those of you with young children may want to use your exercise time to satisfy the demand for mother's time. Take your infant or young child to the park, for a walk around the block, or do some other activity that makes you happy and gives you some exercise at the same time. Parents are particularly creative at "double-timing," doing two things at once without making it look as if that's what you've done.

Older children can be engaged in a game of hop-scotch, jumprope, hide and seek, tag, etc. The list and possibilities are endless. Use your imagination, look at yourself and your family, and then just do something.

If you don't have children, but would like to do something with a child -- borrow one. I'm sure you can talk a neighbor into giving up a child for an hour or two. I know I would have done it gladly when my kids were younger -- I might still do it now that they're teenagers. Maybe you can strike up a deal. You take their youngster off their hands for an hour or two, and they'll answer your business phone so you don't miss any chances to make more money.

TAKE BREAKS

In addition to planned exercise, take a break from the typewriter -- at least 10 minutes out of every hour. Stand up from the chair, take some deep breaths, walk around, do a few neck rolls, wave your arms as if you were trying to kill a swarm of moths, do some stretching exercises, and maybe do a couple of jumping jacks.

This not only relaxes the arms, shoulders, and neck, it

clears the brain. One wise old doctor whom I know says that physical activity gets the blood flowing faster. This in turn pumps more blood to the brain which is why, he says, I can think better after one of these homemade exercise routines. I'll take his word for it.

I don't know if his theory is entirely accurate, but I do know I feel better when I do it. Even when I'm facing a deadline, I stick to this 50 minutes of typing / 10 minutes of flapping-in-the-breeze routine. I make fewer mistakes and get the job done with less wear and tear on my one-of-a-kind human machine.

This same 50/10 schedule, or any modification of it that suits you best, should be followed even if you are physically disabled, if you're medically retired, or restricted in your physical activity in any other way. As soon as you start to feel tired and or your muscles feel tight while typing, TAKE A BREAK.

Stop until the tension goes away. If you're in a wheelchair, for instance, push the chair away from the typewriter, move to another room, look out the window, have a snack (low-calories, now), and try some mental relaxation techniques. When you've got the cobwebs pushed aside, it's time to hit the keys again.

REST UP

There have been lots of articles written on how some people need more or less sleep than others. I read them all, I believe them all, and then I get what MY body and mind seem to ask for. Some nights I get along well on 6 hours; other nights I need 8, 9, or 10 hours of sleep. And sometimes when I take my 10-minute break for relaxation, I find myself taking a short cat-nap.

That's okay! That's why I'm in business for myself. That's one of the things you will enjoy, too. If you need a day off, if you need a few hours for your-self, if you need to sleep-in and be lazy for half a day -- do it. The only one you must answer to or jus-tify this schedule to is YOU. Just be sure you can meet your deadlines.

Allow yourself time to rest. A normal eight-hour day's output is between 35 and 50 pages of double-spaced typing when working from hand-written copy. Normal from transcription may be higher (if you can

157

understand it). Normal output for letters, financial documents, or technical documents will differ. It all depends on what you are capable of doing and how well you can read the customer's work. Don't commit yourself to producing more than you can handle. Schedule breaks and rest periods and even occasional days off. You will need it.

Don't be a worse boss than the one you just had.

HAVE SOME FUN

All work and no play makes the home-based typist:

_____

fill in your own worst idea

After you have eaten right, done enough exercise, taken sufficient breaks, and had adequate rest, try to squeeze in some FUN. That can range from a week in Tahiti to a few hours of gardening and everything in between such as: having lunch with a friend, going to a movie, going camping, window shopping, etc.

On the average of once a week, take time out for YOU. This should be time that is completely separate from family time. If you are single, it should be fairly easy. If you are not single, it may be a little more difficult. But maybe just soaking in the tub for half an hour with the door closed is your idea of luxury and something special. With a little luck and some careful planning you can find time and money for treats -- real ones and mental ones.

Even if your business is barely managing to provide you with a survival income, plan to at least take some time, just a few hours will do -- invent something fun. You know what your interests are, and you know what will give you pleasure. Do it. You worked hard, you earned it. Maybe while you're out having some fun you'll be struck with a fantastic idea to find new clients.

SUMMARY

In summary, eat well but only what you need; keep your body in shape so it can do the very best for you when you depend on it to be there; get enough rest so that you are sharp and alert to do the kind of job your customer is paying for; and enjoy yourself. Be good to your body and mind, and they'll return the favor.

If you do all of that, the maintenance contract on your most expensive (and least expendable) piece of equipment will be renewed by the manufacturer from year to year.

* * * *

Another Peggy P.S.:
You might wonder why this chapter is in a book about how to run a business. The information isn't new, we've all heard it before. BUT, once we become self-employed, our personal health takes on greater significance. Our "sick days" cost us money. I'm not talking here in this chapter about real illnesses, unavoidable accidents, or unplanned misfortunes. No one can predict when those will enter our daily calendar. Rather, this is a prevention chapter to avoid setting ourselves up for trouble and/or failure. I really felt that if I were going to help you prepare yourself to be in business, I ought to tell you all the story that I know, not just the good parts. As obvious as the need for good health is, we often overlook it when we focus on another subject.

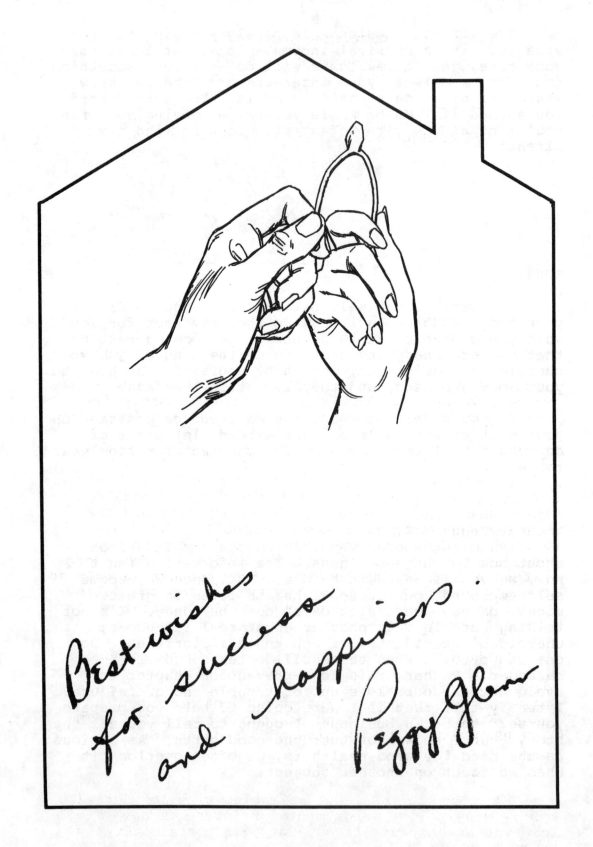

Best wishes
for success
and happiness.
Peggy Glenn

160

CHAPTER 11
Miscellaneous Hints and Tips

This last chapter is a collection of small tidbits of information or advice that somehow didn't fit anywhere else. One by one I've latched onto this advice or learned these lessons or listened to (or read) many stories from other people who have worked at home-based typing businesses. This first section probably deserves a chapter all its own because it's so important.

PROTECTION

Some of you may know that my husband (yes, that darling I've spoken about all through this book) has spent more than 25 years in law enforcement and the fire service (sometimes simultaneously). He's been extremely helpful in alerting me to dangers in our house and in the way I conducted business. We've even written a book on family fire safety because we felt so strongly about it. I picked his brain for the following tidbits. This is very serious advice straight from my heart and I truly hope you take it to heart.

In the 7 years I've been self-employed at home, and in the 4 years I've been corresponding on a regular basis with other people across the country who are also self-employed at home, I've heard some pretty grim tales of loss, damage, and heartache that COULD HAVE BEEN PREVENTED. Please give some thought to:

THEFT PREVENTION

1. Mark all of your valuables with an engraving tool. Many police departments or insurance agents will loan you an engraver free. Use your social security

161

number, birthdate, or driver's license number. Then
record the serial numbers of all of your office equipment and personal valuables on a slip of paper and
store that paper and any receipts or guarantees in a
safe-deposit box. As discussed in the section on insurance, if anything is burned or stolen, you'll be able
to prove you owned it in the first place.

2. Take photographs of all of your belongings --
personal and business -- and store the photos in the
same safe-deposit box. One picture is worth a thousand
ashes or fingerprints.

3. Install dead-bolt locks on your doors -- particularly if you have a sign on your home which advertises your business. As we've already discussed, full-
size office typewriters and office machines are hot
items on the underground resale market (not to mention
all your personal valuables). When installing these
locks, though, remember that you not only want to keep
intruders out, you also want to be able to escape that
home yourself if a fire starts. Don't be imprisoned by
your own security devices.

4. Be careful about mentioning your marital
status if you are single. During that initial telephone call from a potential customer, particularly if
you plan to see customers in the evening, make casual
mention of your father, a brother, or a husband (even
if they live miles away or don't even exist), to dispel
the idea that you are alone and vulnerable to unexpected visits or unnecessary rudeness. We've already
talked about dealing with the fear of strangers enter-
ing your home. The telephone call is one more place
where you can screen out potential problems, and where
you can make it very plain that you are self-assured
and not the kind of person to be pushed around.

One woman wrote to tell me that after what she
thought might have turned into a close call with a customer, she bought a few items of men's clothing, and
strategically located the shoes and dirty socks in the
living room to give the impression of the ever-messy
hubby (I don't have one of those, but some of you
might.) In reality, her husband had been dead for 3
years and she wasn't dating, but she didn't want to
advertise that fact to any customers. She hasn't been
bothered since.

If you're so inclined, take a class in self-
defense. These are offered -- free in many instances

-- by police departments, women's clubs, community colleges, neighborhood groups.

5.   Join the Neighborhood Watch program in your area. This is a nationwide citizens-involvement crime prevention and education unit. If there isn't one in your area, ask how you can help to start one. Statistics prove (and burglars admit) that Neighborhood Watch works! You may also prove to be an asset to your neighborhood simply by virtue of the fact that you work at home during the day. You will find yourself becoming more alert to what should and shouldn't be occurring on your block. What neighbor will ever lodge a complaint against your business if you've saved their home from a burglar? Right!

FIRE SAFETY

6.   Install a smoke detector in your home in close proximity to your "office." These devices are lifesavers as well as property savers. Consider your loss as well as your customers' losses if your "office" area were to have even a small fire. Know what the detector sounds like, and know how to react when the detector goes off, and make sure that everyone else in your home knows how also.

7.   Purchase a multi-purpose, dry-chemical fire extinguisher and know how to use it. Install the extinguisher in the kitchen, on a route away from the most likely source of fire -- the stove.

8.   Prepare an emergency escape plan for your home or apartment in case of fire. Discuss the plan with everyone in your family and walk through the plan if possible. Having a plan eliminates panic and deaths.

9.   Use extension cords sparingly, particularly in your office. If you must use them, make sure they are rated to carry the electrical load. If in doubt, check with an electrician, or read our book, DON'T GET BURNED!

10.   When storing paper, chemicals, or other flammable supplies, be very certain that you don't store them too close to a heat source. Never spread papers on electric range burners.

11.   Walk outside and look at your house or apartment numbers. Are they large, in a contrasting color

from the house, unobstructed by shrubbery, well-lighted
at night? This will make it easier for customers to
find you during the day; it'll also make it easier for
fire and police vehicles to find you in an emergency,
in the dark, from several feet away using only a
spotlight or flashlight.

12.   Do you know the telephone numbers for your
police and fire departments? Is there a sticker on all
your telephones that also identifies your own address
and your own phone number? What if a friend, relative,
houseguest, or client needed to phone for emergency aid
from your home. Would they know your address or phone
number? Would they know the emergency numbers?

LIFE SAFETY

13.   Complete a CPR course, or at least a Red
Cross First Aid course. The information that you will
learn in one of these classes will come in handy when
you least expect it. The 10-15 hours that this will
take will be an investment in your life and possibly
someone else's that can't be measured until you need to
use it.

On the lighter side:

CAR SAFETY

14.   Take a course in basic auto maintenance if
you own a car. If you're entirely non-mechanical (as I
am), at least know how to check the water, air, oil,
brake & transmission fluid, etc. In these days of self-
service gas stations, high-priced gas and repairs, some
preventive maintenance can pay off for you.

Especially in the early stages of your business,
you won't have extra money to be putting into your car.
So baby it, pamper it, and take good care of it so it
will behave until you can give it more high-class attention. This is particularly critical if you will be
offering pick-up and delivery in your business.

Carry flares or portable safety cones in your car,
especially if you travel at night, so that you can
protect yourself or someone else in case of an accident
or mechanical breakdown. Know how to set them out
correctly, and be extremely careful when you get out of
your car to do so.

HOME / APARTMENT MAINTENANCE

15. Take the same kind of course in basic home repairs/maintenance. If such classes are not offered through your community college or adult education department (or if you live some distance from any place to learn this), check into what your library offers. If you find a book that is easy to read, send away for your own copy or order it at your favorite bookstore. The librarian or bookstore owner can help you find out where to send and how much to send if it isn't in stock.

Consider being prepared for something as simple as knowing how to replace a fuse or fix the circuit breaker: Picture yourself facing a deadline in 30 minutes and you blow a fuse or the circuit trips. What customer is going to understand that kind of excuse no matter how true it is? But if you have fixed it, then take the time to tell them about it and impress them with how much you know and how self-sufficient you are. "I met your deadline in spite of this ... that ... or something else!"

MORE EXTRAS YOU CAN OFFER

* Notary Public: A notary public is an official who is authorized to act as a witness for people who sign legal documents. While the fees for this extra service are modest, it doesn't cost you much of anything to be able to offer it.

Each state sets its own rules, regulations, fees, and requirements for becoming a notary. Basically, you must be over 21, a U.S. citizen, a permanent resident of the area in which you will offer notary services, and have no felony convictions.

Write to the Secretary of State in your state's capitol and request an application and copy of the rules and instructions.

* Checkbook Balancing: Five years ago, I would have hired you if you lived in my area. Many people with small businesses are willing to do most of their bookkeeping chores, but they simply hate balancing their bank statements each month. If you can offer this service to your regular customers, you'll be a rare jewel.

* Photocopying: This will involve a financial
investment for a lease or purchase of a copier, but in
some areas could be a big drawing point for your business.

 * Translating: If you live in an area with a high
degree of need for bilingual skills, look around for
opportunities to use them. There are hundreds. This
could range from translating advertisements into a
foreign language, to writing or translating medical
questionnaires for doctors' offices or hosiptals.
There is a professional association of translators.
Write to them for more information if you are interested. Their address is:

        American Translators Association
        P. O. Box 489
        Madison Square Station
        New York, NY 10010

TIMING

        I have a few suggestions regarding when to start
your business. The time of year, the weather, the
trends, and certain scheduling factors can have a bear-
ing on how easily you can implement the processes to
get started.

        These issues are not critical, but if you have a
choice, or if you're able to plan in advance, you can
improve your chances for success by at least considering the following:

 * Academic: It may be wise to start your business
at the beginning of a semester or quarter. If you do
your advertising from early in the term, your name will
be re-occurring in customers' minds. If you are new at
typing academic work, this slow start will allow you to
become familiar with the styles and formats under ideal
conditions rather than under deadline or "rush" conditions.

        The one thing you should be prepared for, however,
is that students frequently wait until the last minute.
The younger students are notorious for this.

 * Business/Commercial: I feel it's best to start
this kind of home-based typing service during good
weather. If your area is subject to snow, lots of

rain, tornadoes, hurricanes, etc., you'll want to have
your customers "wrapped around your finger" by the time
this weather arrives. If you have proven yourself to
be reliable and conscientious and downright G-O-O-D
under ideal conditions, they will be even more grateful
for your services in the poor weather.

     Imagine, for instance, how delighted an insurance
agent would be to have you help out with claims after a
storm after you've given superior service during the
summer. If you handle the situation right, you could
end up with a sizable paycheck based on "rush" or
"hardship" or "emergency" duties. Refer again to my
sample bill in the "Customers" chapter. The items I
listed were for aggravation, but you can also list
items such as: "2 hours in traffic due to blizzard
conditions," or "evening/weekend surcharge for rush
claims processing."

     Be ethical, and be honest, but don't sell yourself
short. You are now a valuable business asset. Charge
for such dedication accordingly.

     * Medical & Legal: These two home-based typing
markets may provide business for you on a year-round
basis, because people get sick without regard to the
calendar, and the courts operate all year long as well.
However, in terms of starting your own business and
building it up to a level that pleases you, it may be
to your advantage to start during a period of good
weather.

     Your advertising may involve a lot of personal
contact, and you want to look your best. This is not
always easy at the height of the rainy season or in 30-
below + wind-chill = 50-below weather. In Houston or
Ft. Lauderdale, looking fresh and professional may not
be possible in the middle of the summer when the humi-
dity index is over 90%, either.

     As I said, some places in the country enjoy good
weather most of the time, so timing may not be a critical factor in a successful start-up. But at least consider your weather, your terrain, your customers, and
your way of life when getting ready to make the big
step to self-employment.

     Careful thought will make the difference between
un-employment, self-employment, and (dread, dread)
re-employment in a "real job."

TWO LOOKS AT REALITY

You do need to face the possibility of slow times or disillusionment. What'll you do if you're having trouble making ends meet? What do you do if you find yourself with a sudden bill and not enough cash to pay for it?

Don't panic!!!!!!!!

Don't get discouraged and start looking for a job!

Don't think that it's all over and you can't make a go of it!

Contact a temporary agency. I did it, and it wasn't really awful. Remember that month-long vacation I told you I took one summer? Well, I over-spent my budget just a little. My MasterCard bill looked as if someone had gone berserk.

When I returned from vacation, there was no work waiting for me. So, I had a friend who was a partner in a new temporary agency. She needed reliable people to fill clients' orders, and I needed about 2 weeks' worth of work. We worked out an agreeable rate for my skills, she found me a job, and I worked at one firm for the whole two weeks.

The first day was painful because I wore pantyhose and a skirt to make a good impression. But after I proved how good I was, I spent the rest of the time in presentable -- but comfortable -- clothes. At the end of the two weeks, I said, "Thanks for the opportunity to work here, it's been fun and I learned some new tricks, I have all the money I need, don't call me, I'll call you."

I haven't gone back since. But it was there when I needed it, and the money came in handy. Besides that, it was a definite ego-booster to know I was still so marketable in the "real world." By going through a temporary agency, I was spared all the formalities, drudgery, and psychic trauma of filling out job applications, going for interviews, etc. It was bearable, and it paid the bills. And no guilt at the end of the 2 weeks!

Lastly, if you give it an honest try, if you do everything "right" and it either doesn't work out or you don't like it, don't consider yourself a failure.

The only failure is failing to try. There is no such
thing as defeat if you at least make an attempt. There
is growth in being able to say, "It's not for me."

PROFESSIONAL GROUPS TO HELP

NATIONAL ASSOCIATION OF SECRETARIAL SERVICES
(N.A.S.S.)
100 Second Avenue South, #604
St Petersburg FL 33701
813/823-3646 or 800/237-1462
FAX 813/894-1277

N.A.S.S. has an excellent newsletter as well as
chapters throughout the country. Although primarily
organized to serve the store-front or office-based
secretarial service, many owners of home-based businesses have told me that they feel welcome and that the
organization meets or exceeds their expectations. Puts
on a conference/workshop annually.

NATIONAL ASSOCIATION OF WOMEN BUSINESS OWNERS
(NAWBO)
500 Michigan Avenue
Chicago IL 60611

NAWBO has chapters throughout the country. Most
members run businesses much more sophisticated than a
home-based typing business, but no one is excluded if
she wants to learn from others and is willing to offer
assistance and expertise where appropriate. Write for
information about the national organization as well as
about any local chapters which may be located near
where you live. Be sure to enclose a courtesy business-
sized SASE. Annual conference, and many regional
meetings/training sessions.

NATIONAL ASSOCIATION
for the
COTTAGE INDUSTRY
P.O. Box 14460
Chicago IL 60614

Mostly an advocacy organization working to make it
easier for all of us to work at home for ourselves or
for someone else. From time to time, they put on an
excellent conference for all cottage-industry owners or
workers. Send an SASE for their latest information.

STAY IN TOUCH WITH ME

If you are particulary pleased with the advice and information in this book, drop me a fan letter. I really do care about making a difference in people's lives. If I made a difference in yours, tell me about it.

If you disagree with something in this book (and if it isn't 10 years from the copyright date), please take a minute to write me a note. I appreciate constructive criticism, and I'll do my best to incorporate your suggestions in future revisions of this book.

You are always welcome to write me asking to be placed on my mailing list. I'll send you the most current information I have on what's going on in the home-based business industry. I stay active in the work-at-home movement, and will usually have pamphlets or information on hand to send to you. Please, please send a business-sized SASE. Provided I'm not retired by the time you read this, I'll be happy to stay in touch.

Peggy Glenn
Typing Business Information
P.O. Box 453
Huntington Beach CA 92648

ANOTHER GREAT RESOURCE

NEW CAREERS CENTER
Business Information Dept
P.O. Box PG-297
Boulder CO 80306
303/447-1087

Among the resources available from here are: "The Whole Work Catalog," which offers books, tapes, and other materials on working from home; and information about a subscription to "The National Home Business Report," a quarterly newsletter devoted to news and tips on working at home.

TWO BOOKS YOU MUST READ!

WORKING FROM HOME by Paul & Sarah Edwards

THE WORK AT HOME SOURCEBOOK by Lynie Arden

NEWSLETTER

One very excellent newsletter for the home-based typist is:

KEYBOARD CONNECTION
P.O. Box 338, Dept. AA
Glen Carbon IL 62034

I have watched this newsletter grow over the last 3 years. The professionalism that is exemplified in this publication is also duplicated in the great articles and wonderful tips for success. Nancy Malvin and Carla Culp, the two women who produce the newsletter still work from their respective homes. Please, when writing for subscription information, enclose a business-sized SASE.

GETTING OUT THE WORD

Below is a letter I used to use when introducing
my typing service to new customers, particularly small
businesses in the area. Feel free to use it as is, or
change it to suit your own style.

The KEY elements are that you:

FIRST, state that you are a **professional**

SECOND, only after you've done the above
do you mention that you work at home.

* * * * * * * * * * * * * * *

ABC Business
123 Profit Drive
Successville US 99999

Good Morning:

Please allow me to introduce myself. My name is
Talented Typist and I am a self-employed, professional,
freelance secretary. I maintain a fully-equipped
office in my home to handle your typing needs.

I would be delighted to visit your office and discuss
the full range of office skills and secretarial
abilities that I provide to businesses such as yours.
Perhaps you can benefit from using my typing service on
either a steady or an intermittent basis.

I'll be calling shortly to arrange a no-obligation half-
hour consultation. If you need assistance immediately,
please call at 123/456-7890.

Sincerely,

Talented Typist

POSTAL ZIP CODE LIST

The following are U.S. Postal Service-approved abbreviations for all 50 states and some territories.

The 2-letter abbreviation should always be used on envelopes. The Postal Service requests that the city name not be abbreviated and that the address be typed in all capital letters. For example:

RIGHT: 924 MAIN STREET
HUNTINGTON BEACH CA 92648

WRONG: 924 Main Street
Hunt. Bch., Cal. 92648

Alabama	AL	Montana	MT
Alaska	AK	Nebraska	NE
Arizona	AZ	Nevada	NV
Arkansas	AR	New Hampshire	NH
California	CA	New Jersey	NJ
Colorado	CO	New Mexico	NM
Connecticut	CT	New York	NY
Delaware	DE	North Carolina	NC
District of Columbia .	DC	North Dakota	ND
Florida	FL	Ohio	OH
Georgia	GA	Oklahoma	OK
Guam	GU	Oregon	OR
Hawaii	HI	Pennsylvania	PA
Idaho	ID	Puerto Rico	PR
Illinois	IL	Rhode Island	RI
Indiana	IN	South Carolina	SC
Iowa	IA	South Dakota	SD
Kansas	KS	Tennessee	TN
Kentucky	KY	Texas	TX
Louisiana	LA	Utah	UT
Maine	ME	Vermont	VT
Maryland	MD	Virginia	VA
Massachusetts	MA	Virgin Islands	VI
Michigan	MI	Washington	WA
Minnesota	MN	West Virginia	WV
Mississippi	MS	Wisconsin	WI
Missouri	MO	Wyoming	WY

In addition, the Postal Service requests that when a street address is not given or is unnecessary, that the city-state-zip code sequence be all on one line.

173

TELEPHONE MESSAGE SLIP SAMPLE

     This is the message-taking slip I designed for my family. I discovered that when I told them what to say and how to say it, I had much better luck with messages. My customers appreciated the thorough way my family takes messages. The impression they created for me was sometimes the first one a customer had of me. In my case as well as in yours, if the message-taker is thorough, courteous, and business-like, it gives my business a great deal of credibility.

     I put a stack of these slips by each phone in the house, not just the phone on my desk. I have yet to miss an important call since I started using these little slips. Feel free to copy them exactly or make modifications to suit your family's style and anything else you would like to know.

```
TYPING CUSTOMER MESSAGE


NAME: _____

PHONE #: _____

MESSAGE: _____

CAN I CALL THEM BACK? _____

WHAT TIME? _____

ANYTHING ELSE? _____

_____

_____

_____

WHO TOOK THE MESSAGE? _____

DAY _____ TIME _____
```

BIBLIOGRAPHY

Below is a comprehensive bibliography of books, magazines, and pamphlets which should provide the answers to any of your business questions. Most of these have already been mentioned in the text of this book, but there are a few new ones, so look closely.

AMERICAN BUSINESS WOMEN'S ASSOCIATION (See page 46)

APA PUBLICATION MANUAL, Publication Sales, American Psychological Association, 1200 Seventeenth, NW, Washington, D. C. 20036.

BEST OF BOTH WORLDS (The), Joan Wester Anderson, Betterway Publications, Inc.

BETTER LETTERS, Jan Venolia, Ten Speed Press.

BLACK'S LAW DICTIONARY, Scribner's, New York.

BUSINESS WRITER'S HANDBOOK (The), Charles T. Brusaw, Gerald J. Alred, & Walter E. Oliu, St. Martin's Press.

COMPLETE GUIDE TO EDITORIAL FREELANCING, C.O'Neill and A. Ruder.

COMPLETE RESUME GUIDE (The), Marian Faux, Monarch Press.

COMPLETE WRITING GUIDE (The), Carolyn Mullins. Prentice-Hall.

CONSUMER INFORMATION CENTER, Pueblo, CO 81009.

THE CRAFT OF FICTION, THE CRAFT OF NON-FICTION, Knott, William C., Reston Publishing Co.

DEAR PUBLISHER, Carol Shrum, P.O. Box 726, Clayton CA 94517 ($4.95)

DENNISON ZIP CODE DIRECTORY.

DOME SIMPLIFIED BOOKKEEPING RECORD #612.

DON'T GET BURNED! A FAMILY FIRE-SAFETY GUIDE, Gary & Peggy Glenn, Aames-Allen Publishing.

DON'T USE A RESUME: USE A QUALIFICATIONS BRIEF, Richard Lathrop, Ten Speed Press.

DORLAND'S ILLUSTRATED MEDICAL DICTIONARY, W. B. Saunders.

EARNING MONEY WITHOUT A JOB, Jay Conrad Levinson, Holt, Rinehart & Winston.

EFFECTIVE SELLING THROUGH PSYCHOLOGY, Victor Buzzota, Wiley-Interscience.

ELEMENTS OF STYLE (The), William Strunk, Jr., & E. B. White, The Macmillan Company.

ENTREPRENEURIAL WOMAN (The), Sandra Winston, Newsweek Books/Bantam.

EXERCISE AND WEIGHT CONTROL, Pamphlet #121H, Consumer Information Center, Pueblo, CO 81009 (60¢).

FAMILY GUIDE TO CRIME PREVENTION, Manuel Estrella,Jr. and Martin Forst, Beaufort Books.

FAMILY WORD FINDER; WRITE BETTER, SPEAK BETTER, Reader's Digest Books, Pleasantville, NY 10570.

555 WAYS TO EARN EXTRA MONEY, Jay Conrad Levinson, Holt, Rinehard & Winston.

FORM AND STYLE, William G. Campbell & Stephen V. Ballou, Houghton Mifflin Company.

HARBRACE COLLEGE HANDBOOK, John C. Hodges & Mary E. Whitten, Harcourt Brace Jovanovich, Inc.

HOME-BASED BUSINESSES, Beverly Feldman, Till Press.

HOW TO ADVERTISE AND PROMOTE YOUR SMALL BUSINESS, G. M.
    Siegel, John Wiley & Sons.

HOW TO GET HAPPILY PUBLISHED, Judith Applebaum.

HOW TO PROSPER IN YOUR OWN BUSINESS, Brian R. Smith,
    Stephen Greene Press.

HOW TO PROTECT YOURSELF FROM CRIME, Ira A. Lipman, Avon
    Books.

HOW TO START, RUN, AND STAY IN BUSINESS, Gregory and
    Patricia Kishel, John Wiley & Sons.

IDEAL GENERAL BUSINESS BOOKKEEPING AND TAX RECORD

LEGAL SECRETARYSHIP, Norma Blackburn, Prentice-Hall.

LITERARY MARKETPLACE, Published by R. R. Bowker Co.,
    available in all libraries.

LITTLE ENGLISH HANDBOOK (The): Choices and
    Conventions, Edward Corbett, John Wiley & Sons.

MANUAL FOR WRITERS OF TERM PAPERS, THESES, AND
    DISSERTATIONS (A), Kate L. Turabian, University of
    Chicago Press.

MEDICAL WORD BOOK (The), Sheila Sloane, W. B. Saunders.

MINDING MY OWN BUSINESS, Marjorie McVicar and Julia
    Craig, Richard Marek Publishers, Inc.

MLA HANDBOOK, Modern Language Association, New York,
    NY.

NEW ENTREPRENEURS (The), Terri and Nona Dawe Tepper,
    Universe Books.

PERSONAL COMPUTER BOOK (The), Peter McWilliams,
    Prelude/Ballantine.

PUBLICITY HANDBOOK, Sperry Hutchinson Company.

PUBLICITY: HOW TO GET IT, Richard O'Brien, Harper &
    Row.

REFERENCE MANUAL FOR STENOGRAPHERS & TYPISTS, Gavin
    Sabin, Gregg/McGraw-Hill.

RESUMES: THE NITTY GRITTY, Joyce Lain Kennedy, Sun
     Features, Inc.

ROGET'S THESAURUS, Norman Lewis (Editor), G. P.
     Putnam's Sons, New York, NY.

SMALL IS BEAUTIFUL, E. F. Schumacher, Harper & Row.

SMALL-TIME OPERATOR (How to Start Your Own Small
     Business, Keep Your Books, Pay Your Taxes, & Stay
     Out of Trouble!), Bernard Kamaroff, CPA, Bell
     Springs Publishing.

SPEAK EASY, Sandy Livner, Summit Books.

STANDARD HANDBOOK FOR SECRETARIES, Lois Hutchinson,
     McGraw-Hill Book Company.

SUPPORT SERVICES ALLIANCE, INC. (see page 46)

SURGICAL WORD BOOK (The), Claudia Tessier, W. B.
     Saunders.

TABER'S CYCLOPEDIC MEDICAL DICTIONARY, Clayton L.
     Thomas, M.D., M.P.H. (Editor), F. A. Davis Co.

TWO-BOSS BUSINESS (The), Elyse and Mike Sommer.

UNDERSTANDING MEDICAL TERMINOLOGY, Sister Agnes Clare
     Frenay, The Catholic Hospital Association, St.
     Louis, MO 63104.

WEBSTER'S COLLEGIATE DICTIONARY, available in book
     stores, colleges, and universities.

WEBSTER'S SECRETARIAL HANDBOOK

WHAT IS ECONOMICS, Jim Eggert, William Kaufmann, Inc.

WOMEN WORKING HOME, Marion Behr and Wendy Lazar, WWH
     Press.

WONDERFUL WRITING MACHINE (The), Bruce Bliven, Random
     House, New York, NY.

WORD PROCESSING BOOK (The), Peter McWilliams,
     Prelude/Ballantine.

WORD PROCESSORS AND INFORMATION PROCESSING, Dan
     Poynter, Para Publishing.

WORDS OFTEN MISSPELLED AND MISPRONOUNCED, Ruth Gleeson
     Gallagher and James Colvin.

WORKING MOTHER MAGAZINE.

WORKING WOMAN MAGAZINE.

WRITE RIGHT! Jan Venolia, Periwinkle Press/Ten Speed
     Press.

WRITER'S HANDBOOK, The Writer.

WRITER'S MARKET, Writer's Digest Books.

     I know there are at least 300-400 more excellent
books out there that will help you with any aspect of
your business. This list represents only those books
I've read myself or which have been highly recommended
by my closest business colleagues. Check your local
library for copies, check your favorite neighborhood
bookstore, check in the large chain bookstores. If you
have any trouble locating one of these books, ask the
public librarian or bookstore clerk to help you look it
up in Books in Print, the book that lists all books in
print. If the book you want is no longer "in print"
write directly to the publisher for more information.

     Good reading, best of luck with your business. I
hope you've enjoyed this book as much as I've enjoyed
writing it for you. Type it with pride!

INDEX

Please try to find this book in your local bookstore or in a catalog that sells books to home-based business owners before you order directly from us. These dealers work very hard to support all the books we publish, and we'd prefer you buy from us only as a last resort. Support your local bookstore, please.

If you checked this copy out of the library, please do not tear out the order coupon. Please carefully photocopy the page and leave the order form intact in the book.

You may also order the companion volume to this book, but there is no need to have both. If you own neither, choose between the two. If you own this one, there's no need to buy the other.

ORDER FORM

TO: Aames-Allen Publishing Co.
        Typing Business Information
        P.O. Box 453
        Huntington Beach CA 92648

FROM: _____
        Name

        _____
        Address

        _____
        City/State/Zip

        _____
        Phone Number in case we need to confirm above

Please send me the following:

____   WORD PROCESSING PROFITS AT HOME $15.95
____   MAKING MONEY TYPING AT HOME   13.95

        TOTAL FOR MERCHANDISE   _____

        Plus 6-1/4% tax for Californians   _____

        Plus $2 shipping each item   _____

        TOTAL ENCLOSED (check or money order) $_____